Y0-AGT-642

IMMORTALS OF SCIENCE

HIPPOCRATES ARISTOTLE
EUCLID ARCHIMEDES
LEONARDO COPERNICUS
GALILEO KEPLER HARVEY
DESCARTES BOYLE NEWTON
PRIESTLEY LAVOISIER GAUSS
FARADAY DARWIN MENDEL
PASTEUR MAXWELL KOCH
ROENTGEN PLANCK CURIE
RUTHERFORD

The Science Wall of Honor on the Charles A. Dana Hall of Science at the University of Bridgeport, Connecticut. This memorial was created to commemorate and perpetuate the names of the world's Immortals of Science whose fundamental discoveries in the field of natural science have yielded the greatest benefits to mankind's fund of knowledge and continue to improve its way of life. A world-wide poll was taken among leading scientists, educators and editors to select the names of the first twenty-five Immortals whose names are inscribed on this handsome wall.

ROBERT KOCH
Father of Bacteriology

Scissors-cut silhouette of Koch
about the year 1890

Robert Koch

IMMORTALS OF SCIENCE

ROBERT KOCH

Father of Bacteriology

by DAVID C. KNIGHT

Pictures by Gustav Schrotter

FRANKLIN WATTS, INC.
575 Lexington Avenue, New York 22

SECOND PRINTING

Library of Congress Catalog Card Number: 61–7501

© Copyright 1961 by Franklin Watts, Inc.

Printed in the United States of America

For Gisela

Contents

Dr. Robert Koch
Writes a Letter

ONE April evening in the year 1876, a young German doctor whose practice was in East Prussia sat down to write a letter. It was a letter that was destined to change the young doctor's career—a career that would make him a rescuer of diseased lives the world over.

Dr. Robert Koch looked older than his real age, which was thirty-three. A few years before, he had grown the full beard that he was to wear for the rest of his life. Before picking up his pen to write, he methodically took off his gold-rimmed spectacles and polished them.

When he replaced the spectacles, the bridge settled comfortably into the fold of skin that seemed to grow deeper as the years wore on. The spectacles gave the young physician an owlish look. Dr. Robert Koch had always been very nearsighted.

Around Koch was a strange world indeed—but a world that he loved and had built himself. Actually, it was just a curtained-off portion of his own consultation office. Everywhere stood bottles, test tubes, and beakers of dark-looking liquids. Under covered jars stood his cultures in which deadly germs had been carefully grown. On the far table were his microscope and the incubator he had made himself to keep his germs at just the right temperature. Here, too, were the thin slivers of wood he used to transfer infected material from one white mouse to another.

Perhaps no other corner of a private office was later to mean so much to a suffering world. For it was in this cramped, weird-looking "laboratory" that Robert Koch dedicated himself to the investigation of communicable disease—the deadly world of microscopically small organisms that could spread death to much larger ones.

Dr. Koch dipped his pen in the ink, but still he did not write. The pen hovered over the paper as Koch's professional conscience began to bother him again.

There was no need to remind himself that he was District Physician of the township of Wollstein. Wollstein had some 4000 inhabitants and Koch's job was to look after their health. In the next village, there was a peasant woman whose baby was due at any hour; right now Koch should have been on his way jogging over the country roads to check up on her. A farm child, ten miles away in the opposite direction, had the croup. A forester on the outskirts of Wollstein had cut his leg badly with an ax the day before. Had infection set in since Koch had dressed the wound? A carpenter's wife lay very still on her bed not five streets away from where Koch was sitting. He knew that she would not last out the week, for she had the dreaded disease, tuberculosis.

Robert Koch sighed. Sick, in pain, even dying—his patients would all have to wait. The letter to Dr. Ferdinand Cohn at the Botanical Institute in Breslau must be written tonight. Cohn was one of the greatest bacteriologists in Germany, and Koch had something important to tell him.

Doubtful that the famous man would even read a letter from an obscure country doctor, Koch began the letter anyway. He started it with the words, "Esteemed Herr Professor . . ."

> Stimulated by your work on bacteria . . . , I have for some time been at work on investigations of anthrax. . . . After many vain attempts, I have finally been successful in discovering the process of development of the anthrax bacillus. . . . Before I bring this into the open I respectfully appeal to you, Esteemed Herr Professor, as the foremost authority on bacteria, to give me your judgment regarding this discovery. . . .
>
> I respectfully request you to permit me to show you, within the next few days, at the Botanical Institute, the essential experiments.
>
> Should you . . . be willing to grant my humble request, will you kindly appoint the time when I may come to Breslau?
>
> With the highest esteem,
>
> > Yours respectfully,
> > R. Koch,
> > District Physician.

On the morning of April 22, 1876, Dr. Ferdinand Cohn strode into the Botanical Institute at Breslau, murmured "Good morning" to his laboratory assistants, and entered his private office. On his desk was a letter postmarked from a town called Wollstein near the Polish border.

Cohn picked the letter up, tore it open and, at first, read it with some interest. Then a slow smile broke at the corners of his mouth.

Up to this time, no scientist had ever seen the complete life cycle of a germ—or microbe—unfold before his eyes. True, several young men had claimed some such discovery or other but they had never been able to prove it.

Nevertheless, Cohn spoke to a number of doctors at the Institute about the matter. Then he sent a letter off to the young District Physician, telling him to be at the Botanical Institute on April 30 to demonstrate his experiments.

In the days that followed, Dr. Cohn idly wondered who this Koch might be. Was his only another mistaken "discovery"? Or would the country doctor really have something to show them?

Harz Mountain Boyhood

SEVERAL hardy generations of Kochs had lived in or near the small town of Clausthal in the province of Hanover before Robert Hermann Heinrich Koch was born on December 11, 1843. Robert was the third son of Hermann and Mathilde Koch.

Clausthal was a pleasant little town in the famous Harz Mountains region of central Germany. Robert might well have been the son of a forester for the Harz range is one of the most deeply wooded in Europe. The Upper Harz, however, is rich in silver, iron, lead, and copper and Hermann Koch, Robert's father, had become a miner.

But Hermann Koch did not remain an ordinary miner for long. He had always lived a hard life, working first in the mines of his native Germany, then in those of France, then shifting back to Germany again to mine the rich deposits of silver near Clausthal. Though he had had little education, Hermann was a forceful and intelligent man; he determined to work his way up in the mining industry. As time went on, he rose step by step to become director of a mining company. This position carried with it the sought-after title of *Bergrath,* or expert mining engineer. Later, he became an advisor on mining affairs to the Prussian government.

Yet even with the title and salary of *Bergrath,* Hermann Koch was hard put to provide for his large family. By 1856, Frau Koch had given birth to her thirteenth child. Clothing them all was no easy matter. There were eleven boys in the Koch family, and coats and pants, when they became outgrown, were regularly passed down from the eldest to the youngest. Thus, when Robert, or his older brothers Adolf or Wilhelm wore theirs out, the younger boys had to wear garments that were patched out of all resemblance to the originals.

Frau Koch found that feeding her large family was an even more serious problem. She was, however, a woman with a deep sense of family honor. Mathilde Koch refused to run into debt, even if it meant that her children

Number 555, Osteroder Strasse, Clausthal (at right), the house where Robert Koch was born.

ate only bread with nothing on it. Indeed, this often happened. But there were other times, too, when there was a bit of extra money in the family purse. On such days, the Koch children had black bread and milk for breakfast; vegetables and milk-soup at noon; more black bread and perhaps an apple in the afternoon; and bread, cheese, and milk for supper. Only on Sunday was white bread put on the table, and only twice a week could Frau Koch afford to serve meat.

The Koch children knew such luxuries as coffee and tea only by name. Sugar, too, was something they had heard of but had never tasted.

Although there might have been a lack of food and clothing in the Koch family, there was seldom a lack of fun. In 1855, Hermann Koch had been able to buy back the very house his own father had been forced to sell years before. In the rear of the rambling old home on the Kronenplatz was an orchard where Robert and his brothers and sisters played hide-and-seek and robbers-and-princes. In the Kronenplatz itself there always seemed to be a game of hopscotch in progress.

In the evening, when Hermann Koch came home from a hard day's work in the mines, he often spent an hour with his children—an hour that they loved. After supper he would smoke his wooden pipe and tell them fairy tales, or his own adventures traveling about when he was young. Robert especially listened spellbound to these stories. Probably he never forgot them, for they were to form the basis of a lifelong desire—to see and know distant lands.

As early as 1848, Herr and Frau Koch suspected that in

Robert they had an unusually bright son. For five-year-old Robert seemed to have learned to do an amazing thing. He could read a newspaper! And as the years passed, Robert showed an increasing interest in the things of nature about him.

Growing up in the thick, wooded slopes of the Harz Mountains was a perfect atmosphere for a scientist-to-be. For one thing, the outdoor life built up in Robert a rugged physique and unusual powers of endurance—qualities he would later need for a long life of scientific work. For another, there was the teeming world of nature about him to study and enjoy.

Robert loved best to roam over the Harz Mountains armed with a book on natural history, a bottle of alcohol, and pins and boxes in search of insects, stones, and plants. Later, he would return with his specimens and add them to the little museum he had set up in his room. At any moment, he might drop everything to investigate something that interested him: how an ant's feelers were made, why a seed pod burst, how the eye of a fly was built.

One of Koch's brothers later wrote of him: "While we gave our time to youthful games, Robert devoted his to nature study. His favorite occupation was to examine moss and lichen with a magnifying glass and to study all kinds of animals."

Yes, Robert *did* have a "magnifying glass." One day he had been rummaging around in a battered chest belonging to his father, and had discovered an old pocket lens. True, it was a little scratched, but Robert snatched it up at once and went to Hermann Koch.

"Please, Father," Robert began, "may I have this to study my specimens?"

Hermann Koch looked at his son and smiled. With growing interest, he had watched his son's fascination with nature. Wisely, he had always let Robert go his own way. He would do the same now.

"Take the lens and use it well," said Hermann Koch.

Robert did. A whole new world seemed to unfold as he held the old, scratched lens over his flowers and leaves and lichens and insects. It was a world he had not known existed. Here was how the things of nature were really put together.

Often to the Koch household came Robert's favorite uncle, Eduard Biewend, who was Mathilde Koch's brother. An intelligent and sensitive man, Dr. Biewend had a wide knowledge of nature and wild life. On each visit he encouraged and stimulated young Robert in his nature studies. Many times Dr. Biewend took his nephew on hikes through the green Harz forests, pointing out examples of animal life and collecting insect and mineral specimens. Often accompanying them would be Dr. Biewend's own son, Robert. This cousin of Robert Koch's was a year younger than himself, and had come to live with the Koch family. The two cousins became fast friends; later, Robert Biewend was to marry Robert Koch's younger sister, Helene.

Among Dr. Biewend's many interests was the comparatively new science of photography. It was from this uncle that Robert first learned to make pictures by *daguerreotype*—an early photographic process using copper plates covered with silver. Later, this knowledge was to prove of great value to Koch in his microscopic work.

Meanwhile, in 1851, Robert had entered the Clausthal *gymnasium,* or high school, where he proved to be an alert student. His teachers learned early that Robert was especially good in mathematics and all subjects dealing with nature. But he had a talent for learning languages, too, studying Latin, Greek, and French. He also studied English, which he later learned to speak quite well.

Two of Robert's hobbies were playing the piano and the *zither,* a small, flat-stringed instrument. While he loved music, he soon discovered a third hobby that completely fascinated him. It was the game of chess. Again, it was his uncle, Dr. Biewend, who introduced him to this pastime. There was something exciting and challenging to Robert about chess; he mastered the game so well that he became champion of the Clausthal gymnasium. Nor did this passionate love of chess ever seem to weaken. On dangerous medical expeditions in later life, he would play the game for relaxation in the steaming jungles of Africa and in the shadow of the Egyptian pyramids.

These school years passed quickly for Robert. Discipline at the gymnasium was strict, and his teachers were demanding. But between his schoolwork and his rambles for specimens through the Harz Mountains Robert was learning much. Soon it was Eastertime of 1862 and he was ready to take his *Abitur*—the final examination for graduation from the gymnasium. With four other students, Robert had to write a theme about the mythical hero, Ulysses. He surprised his teachers by handing in a three-page, satisfactory paper in a very short time. In English, mathematics, physics, history, and geology, Robert received grades of "very good."

The pleasant boyhood days in the Harz Mountains were over. Robert knew that the serious business of earning a living lay ahead. Secretly he hoped that his future would lead him to the distant lands he longed to see.

THREE

Koch Goes to Göttingen

THE Koch family had been short of money for so long that there was little thought of sending even one of their sons to a university. Already, both of Robert's older brothers had left home to seek their fortunes in America. Robert thought many times of doing the same, for the urge to travel was still strong in his mind. Perhaps, thought Hermann Koch, who understood this urge, Robert might try to become a traveling merchant and sail about the world.

Mathilde Koch, however, was against such ideas. Having lost two sons to a foreign land, she refused to lose Robert too, for he was her favorite. Thus it was decided that Robert would go into some sort of business, perhaps starting as an apprentice in the shoe trade.

Then, suddenly, just as Robert graduated from the gymnasium at the head of his class, the Koch family's fortunes changed for the better. Some property had come into the family, and Hermann Koch made up his mind that his promising son should have a university education.

Robert said that he wanted to go to the famous University of Göttingen, and that was where he was enrolled. A few short days after he graduated from the gymnasium,

Koch arrives at Göttingen.

he packed up the few clothes he owned and started out for the old University town in west central Germany.

When he arrived, the country boy from the Harz was thrilled. Compared to little Clausthal, Göttingen was a city of some size. Everywhere there was bustle and activity. Young men in students' caps roamed arm-in-arm through the streets, others strolled with girls along the lovely Leine River. Fascinated, Robert headed toward the spires of the University, lugging his trunk with him.

Once in his quarters, Robert unlocked his trunk and flipped open the lid. He stared at the contents, first stunned, then ashamed. Bright clots of purple crisscrossed the laundry his mother had so carefully pressed for him. The bottle of ink he had wedged into the trunk at the last minute had somehow broken and spilled over his clothes.

A nearby classmate, seeing the serious, bespectacled Koch peering down at the catastrophe, burst into laughter.

Robert looked up and then began to laugh too. After all, what did a few stained clothes matter? Here, at Göttingen, he could see and hear famous scientists, he could study to his heart's content. Here, too, he would be able to look through a real microscope instead of a scratched pocket lens.

For Robert had come to the University for one purpose only—to study. And that is what he did. Some students might spend their time drinking in the taverns. Others of the famous "Student Corps" might go about dueling with swords and scarring each other's faces as marks of "courage." Not young Koch—there was too much to do, too much to learn about.

Still, Robert could not seem to forget the colorful tales of his father's wanderings. He still longed to visit the foreign lands, see the strange animals and stones and plants he had so often read about. What, Koch began to ask himself, could he study at Göttingen that would make a life of travel possible?

After he had spent about a year at the University, Koch had the answer. He was more interested in natural science than he was in mathematics or Greek or Latin, for these might only lead to a teaching career. It was the study of insects, plants, and animals that interested him most. And —were not these studies more or less related to the science of *medicine?* Robert decided to take up medicine so that he could become, perhaps, an army doctor and serve in foreign lands.

Once this plan had taken shape in his mind, Robert plunged into his university studies with great determination. So hard did he work that he had little time left now for his botanical excursions, except on occasional Sundays. Often, as the years passed, he would even cut short his holidays at Clausthal so that he could hurry back to Göttingen and his medical books.

Although Koch was to become one of the great pioneers in the new science of *bacteriology*—the study of very small plant organisms—he wrote in later life that he was not especially drawn to such studies while he was at the University. Instead, it was his sense of curiosity and investigation—a burning urge to find out about things— that was aroused at Göttingen. In large part, this was due to his teachers there.

Fortunately for young Koch, Göttingen had attracted

to its lecture halls a number of excellent professors—men who represented perhaps the most brilliant scientific minds gathered together in one place in the world. There were, for example, Friedrich Woehler, the chemist; Wilhelm Krause, the pathologist; the great clinician, K. E. Hasse, and the well-known physiologist, Georg Meissner. Karl Friedrich Gauss, perhaps the greatest mathematician of his time, was also at Göttingen. Besides these men, Robert Koch heard lectures on trigonometry by H. Ulrich, on physics from Wilhelm Weber, on botany by F. Griese-bach. Robert never ceased to wonder that all of these talented men were assembled in a spot just twenty-five miles from his own home town of Clausthal. The young scientist-to-be lost no opportunity to learn all he could from each of them.

But there was still another teacher at Göttingen who, above all others, helped to shape Robert's career and mold his character for his later work. This man was the famous anatomist, Jacob Henle.

It was Henle's influence that undoubtedly started young Koch on his lifelong study of very small organisms. Twenty years before, Jacob Henle had written a famous book on communicable—contagious, or "catching"—diseases. When this book was written, only a few people dreamed that tiny living plants (called *bacteria*)—so tiny that they could only be seen under a microscope—could cause a communicable disease. What Henle was saying was what we know to be true today; namely, that one person infected with a disease can give it to another, either by direct contact with the other person, or by the other person's coming in contact with an object that the infected person has touched.

Henle had also written these famous words in his book: "Before microscopic forms can be regarded as the cause of contagion in men, they must be constantly found in the contagious material; they must be isolated from it and their strength tested."

Little did Professor Henle suspect that the nearsighted young man who listened so carefully to his lectures, and who peered so intently through the microscope in the laboratory, was to take these words and make them into one of the cornerstones of scientific medicine.

Meanwhile, Robert was doing his first real experimenting with animals. Professor Meissner, an expert in this field, took a liking to young Koch and taught him the techniques of *inoculation*—introducing small doses of tiny organisms into the tissues of living animals. And Professor Hasse gave him instruction in *pathology*—the science of treating diseases, finding out what their natures are, and determining what causes them. Almost thirty years later, Hasse remembered Koch as a "thin, pale young man with a quiet, observant nature."

But Robert Koch also proved early that he could be an original thinker. In June, 1864, Professor Henle suggested to his medical students that a prize be given to one of them who—in ten months' time—could solve a then-unanswered anatomical problem. Koch at this time was working under Wilhelm Krause, head of the University's Pathological Institute. In February of the following year—before the ten months were up—Robert presented to

Krause what he thought might be the solution to the problem. Across the top of the paper he wrote the Latin words *Nunquam otiosis,* which he had adopted as his motto. Indeed, the words suited the busy Koch, for they meant "never idle."

To Robert's surprise and delight, he won first prize in the contest. The reward was eighty thalers (about sixty dollars)—a good sum of money in 1865. Koch was particularly pleased to receive this money because now he could return for another semester at Göttingen without having to ask his father for tuition money.

Aware that his father had been worrying about this, Robert wrote him that: "When I was home last, you did not show much appreciation for my knowledge in the field of medicine. But sometimes it happens that even a blind hen finds a kernel of corn. This has been the case with me. I have won the first prize of our school of medicine this year."

As an additional reward for winning Henle's contest, Koch was made a full-fledged assistant in the Museum of Pathology. Now twenty-two, Robert began work on his doctor's thesis, which he would have to present to his professors for graduation. He set to work to investigate the origin of certain fatty acids in the human body.

One way, thought the enthusiastic Koch, that he could really find out about such acids was to use himself as a guinea pig. Thus he started eating half a pound of pure butter a day! After the fifth day, however, he became so sick that he decided to confine his experiments to animals alone.

Nevertheless, it was on this bit of work that Robert prepared and submitted to the University authorities his doctor's thesis in January of 1866. He graduated with honors.

While the young doctor was still haunted by his old desire to see the world, a new longing had also taken hold of him. This was to see and know another sort of world—the scientific world of the unseen—the only passport to which was a microscope.

Koch was to explore both worlds, but it was to be the mysterious, unseen one that drew him first.

FOUR

Berlin

SHORTLY after his graduation from Göttingen, Robert Koch decided to do postgraduate work in Berlin. Finding an inexpensive apartment near the large Charity Hospital, he moved in and soon became enchanted with the beauty and cosmopolitan atmosphere of the busy German capital.

Koch immediately enrolled as an intern in the Charity Hospital where he looked forward eagerly to hearing lectures by the famous pathologist, Rudolf Virchow.

Yet, the longer the young physician stayed in Berlin, the more disappointed he became. Much as he loved the city, conditions at the Charity Hospital were hopelessly overcrowded; over 4000 patients crammed the rooms— to say nothing of the large number of young doctors doing their intern work there. In the packed clinics and lecture halls, Robert could scarcely hear what was being said, let alone see the various operations being performed in the theaters. It was not at all like Göttingen where he had been used to giving his full attention to individual patients. Then, too, many of the interns were ahead of Koch in their studies; often these were the only ones allowed to examine patients.

Koch also found that living in the capital city was more expensive than he had thought. Nevertheless, he decided to stay on in Berlin at least until Easter and learn all he could from the famous Virchow.

Meanwhile, his future career began to worry him. What would he do with himself and where would he settle down to practice medicine? The thought of becoming just another country doctor in Germany did not appeal to Koch in the least.

Once again, the thought entered his mind of obtaining a commission as an army doctor. Then he might be able to serve in some foreign city. Just what country's army he might be attached to did not much matter to Koch. In fact, he applied to the Russian legation for such a position and was refused. The situation seemed to be the same wherever he went. At the moment, Europe was not at war, armies were at peacetime strengths, and such posts were hard to find. Koch finally gave up this idea in favor of another plan that he had often considered.

Why not become, for a time, a ship's doctor? Surely by serving aboard one of the great ocean-going steamers he could both gain medical experience and satisfy his urge to travel. Other doctors, with whom he talked at the Charity Hospital, encouraged Koch in this plan.

Full of enthusiasm, Robert wrote his family in Clausthal, asking them what they thought of the idea. "Let me know soon about this," his letter concluded, "so that I can begin immediately to look about for such a post."

Mathilde Koch was shocked when she learned what her favorite son meant to do. Tears in her eyes, she appealed to her husband:

"Is it not enough that two sons have already gone to America?" she said. "And now—lose a third to Heaven knows where? No, Hermann, I won't permit it. Write him! Write him immediately and get this nonsense out of his head."

Herr Koch did indeed write Robert. But it was an understanding, man-to-man letter that he did not show to his wife.

"My dear son," it went, "can a man as old as I really advise you what to do? Each man holds the key to his own future and must be responsible for what he decides to do. When you think something is right, then do it! But whatever you decide to do, you will do it well—even at home. Weigh your choice carefully."

Mathilde Koch, however, suspected that her husband had written something of this sort; she knew Hermann well. She decided to influence Robert's decision with a maneuver of her own. Robert had a sweetheart in the town of Clausthal. Her name was Emmy Adolphine Josephine Fraatz.

Tiny, vivacious Emmy was the youngest daughter of a leading town official who was also a Lutheran minister. Since the two young people wrote each other regularly, Frau Koch had but to drop by the parsonage and make known Robert's new plans. Emmy, who wanted a husband who would stay at home in Germany, would bring her influence to bear either in her next letter to Robert or when he came home for the Easter holidays.

Emmy decided to wait till Eastertime, when the young couple met again after Robert's absence of many weeks. As children, Emmy and Robert had played together countless times—often she would pretend to be the captive princess who would be saved by Robert in the nick of time from fierce robbers. Later, they had attended village dances together, and gone on picnics where Robert would poach eggs for the young ladies. Often, they strolled in the Harz forests, with Emmy listening fascinated as Robert talked of the many things in nature around them. Soon they became more than just companions; they fell in love.

When he saw Emmy again, Robert knew that he had a decision to make. He knew it, too, when he looked into his mother's eyes; they were red from crying for fear he would leave his native Germany.

Encouraged as he had been with his father's letter, Robert had been thinking over one sentence in that letter. "Whatever you decide to do, you will do it well—*even at home.*"

Under this strong family influence, and that of his bride-to-be, Koch gave up the idea of being a ship's doctor. After all, he wanted Emmy for his wife—and wives of ships' doctors could not go on long sea voyages with their husbands.

A few days later, Robert Koch and Emmy Fraatz announced that they were engaged.

Back went Robert to Berlin to complete his course under Virchow. There he received an offer of an assistantship in the General Hospital at Hamburg—provided he first passed his state examination to practice medicine. This he did in March in the city of Hanover.

It was to be in Hamburg then—*at home* in Germany—that he was to make his way as a doctor of medicine.

FIVE

Hamburg

ROBERT KOCH easily located rooms near the General Hospital in the old Hanseatic city of Hamburg. The young doctor found much there to occupy his attention, especially research work that allowed him to satisfy some of his curiosity with the microscope.

About this time an epidemic of the disease called *cholera* had broken out in Hamburg. Only seven short years before the same disease had claimed nearly two thousand lives in that city. Hamburg, being a busy port city on the North Sea, nearly always fell victim to outbreaks of cholera, for infected sailors would bring the germ with them from the Orient and other distant places. This time, however, the disease seemed to have been transported by way of land, probably from recent war areas in southeastern Europe.

Little was known about cholera in 1866, and doctors were far from having developed a successful vaccination against it. All that was known was that it seemed to be transmitted by polluted food and water. Symptoms included diarrhea, vomiting, extreme weakness, and finally complete collapse. And whenever a cholera epidemic struck a community the death rate was always high.

This killer disease had haunted the civilized world for centuries, and Koch welcomed an opportunity to study it. Hundreds of Hamburg citizens had become infected with cholera and many were brought to the General Hospital where some came under Koch's care.

That terrible spring, the diseased material from victims passed many times under the polished lens of Koch's microscope. The serious young intern examined it with great interest, little knowing that seventeen years later he would successfully isolate and conquer the deadly microbe.

There is evidence, however, that even in 1866 Koch was showing signs of medical genius. Notes and drawings in Koch's own hand were found decades later showing that he must have seen the cholera germ itself. At the time, however, young and inexperienced, he did not as yet realize the meaning of what he saw.

Besides, Robert had other things on his mind in the spring of 1866. He wanted to marry Emmy as soon as possible; but for that he needed much more money than he made at the General Hospital in Hamburg. As an intern, he had little opportunity to develop a private practice to gain extra income.

In addition, his old urge to travel to distant lands still gnawed at him. Despite his promises to his family and bride-to-be, he could not seem to get rid of this longing. Just walking along the famous Alster with the smell of salt air in his nostrils was enough to bring visions of exotic places crowding into his mind. Sailormen from all over the world thronged the streets of Hamburg. Great steamers and sailing ships with their lure of foreign ports and high adventure jammed the harbor. Staring enviously

at these ships and men, Koch's pulse would beat just a little faster.

Tiny Emmy Fraatz, however, still at home in Clausthal,
suspected the temptations that Hamburg was putting in
Robert's way. It was all very well that they wrote loving
letters back and forth, but—still—a letter was just a letter
and no substitute for seeing each other in person. Emmy
decided to take no chances on losing Robert; somehow
she would visit him in Hamburg.

However, a young lady could not travel alone to Hamburg to visit a young man—even if that man were her
fiancé. Emmy needed an excuse to visit the city—and soon
a good one came along. Robert's favorite uncle, Dr. Biewend, also lived in the big port city and had never met his
nephew's bride-to-be. Somehow, Emmy wangled an invita-
tion and took a train for Hamburg. There, of course, she
also visited Robert.

The hard-working young doctor was surprised but glad,
too, to see his fiancée. He had missed Emmy and he told
her so. Eagerly they talked over their plans for the future.

One warm evening they strolled down by the harbor.
Lights were blazing all over the dark water, and once
again the smell of the sea air made Koch's head swim.
Soon the pair came to the busy pier of St. Pauli where a
great oceangoing steamer was making ready to put out to
sea. Men and women, carrying trunks and leading children, were going aboard the big vessel. They were clearly
emigrants, leaving Germany for South America.

"How I envy them!" said Robert suddenly. "They will
be finding a new life in a new land. Think of the adventures they will have."

Koch and Emmy on the St. Pauli pier in Hamburg.

Emmy did not reply. True, the strong young men climbing the gangplank were full of courage and hope. It was their wives and their parents left on the pier that Emmy was looking at. In their eyes were tears at leaving their homeland.

"Emmy," Robert burst out, completely under the spell of the scene, "why can't we do the same? We can find a new life too, perhaps in the South Seas. Oh, we needn't go right away of course," he added. "It will take a few weeks to plan and pack . . . I'm sure we can make a go of it. Trust me. Will you go?"

Emmy turned slowly and looked up at Robert. Koch thought that perhaps he had convinced her.

"If you love me," she said briefly, "you must stay here at home."

Looking at this fresh young girl whom he loved, Koch knew that she had given him his choice. It was either the sea and faraway lands, or Emmy. He could not have both.

Koch chose Emmy.

"As soon as I can," Robert said quietly, "I will look for a practice of my own. Then we'll be married."

Restless Years

SINCE there was little opportunity for Robert Koch to increase his income at the General Hospital in Hamburg, he resigned in September, 1866. At home in Clausthal again, he awaited the results of a number of applications he had sent out to other institutions.

Robert did not have to wait long. In October, he was offered a position as resident physician in a hospital for the mentally ill in the little town of Langenhagen near Hanover. In addition to his regular duties, Koch also had the opportunity to build up a private practice among the townspeople and peasants around Langenhagen. The young physician proved popular with his patients and his practice grew. Soon he was able to buy a horse with which he could more easily make his rounds. By spring of the following year, Robert could write Emmy that he was now making enough to support a wife.

On July 16, 1867, the couple was married in their native Clausthal. Emmy's father, the Reverend Fraatz, performed the ceremony in his own church. Robert then took his bride to the seven-room apartment he had rented in Langenhagen. Koch's practice continued to thrive and presently he added a carriage to his equipment.

Now twenty-three, Robert Koch was a settled, married man who, for the time being at least, had given up all thought of romantic trips around the world. But there was still left to him that other world—the world of the microscopically small—where no one could forbid him to enter. So once more, in the few hours he could spare from his practice, he took up his study of tiny organisms. Emmy proved to be a big help to him. Industriously, she would gather all sorts of specimens from lakes, ponds, and swamps for Robert to examine under his microscope.

Koch's stay in Langenhagen, however, was to last but a bare two years. Due to a change in directors of Koch's hospital—and also for reasons of economy—he was told that unfortunately they could no longer afford a resident physician. Koch understood and once again began the search for a new post.

More and more, Robert was beginning to know what kind of position he wanted most. Specifically, he wanted to settle down in a place where—at one and the same time—he could practice medicine *and* carry on his microscopic investigations.

By the end of August, 1868, he believed he had found such a place. This was in another small town called Niemegk near Postdam. Here, in September, his daughter Gertrude was born. The little girl was to be his only child and, throughout his life, he doted on her.

Niemegk, too, was not to hold Koch for long. He soon discovered that many people there preferred to be treated by cheap, unscientific methods that were administered by men who were not real doctors. Koch promptly packed up and left within a year.

The young physician next accepted a practice in another small town called Rakwitz. This town was in the Province of Posen and not far from the Polish border. Rakwitz had scarcely three thousand people, but in the outlying countryside there were many more who would need the services of a doctor. Koch then rented a large two-story house, in which was also housed the local post office, and settled down to his new practice.

At first, few patients came to Dr. Koch's office. Moreover, he was unable to communicate with some of those who did come. Rakwitz was near the border of Russian-controlled Poland and many of its citizens spoke only Polish. Thus, for those patients who did not speak German, Koch was forced to hire an interpreter. In spite of this, the practice did not seem to grow in the weeks that followed.

Then one day Koch was called to the house of one of Rakwitz' wealthy citizens. This man, a wealthy landowner, had accidentally wounded himself with a revolver. Koch deftly treated the wound and the man recovered. The word then went around that young Dr. Koch was a trustworthy, even brilliant physician, and from then on his practice increased.

Not only had Koch now become "accepted," he became an absolute favorite with the whole community. Quiet and serious, yet displaying an unexpected sense of humor, he became Rakwitz' beloved "Herr Doktor." He also became the good friend of the local druggist and the town mayor. Often he would drop into the local tavern to discuss the affairs of the day with them—and also speculate on whether Chancellor Bismarck would make war with

France. There were many invitations, too, to visit neighbors. Everywhere Koch went he was greeted with a good word, for he in turn had one for everyone else.

During this period, too, Koch's home environment was perhaps the happiest of his life. Again, he was at work with his microscope. Emmy, glad to be settled at last with her family, cheerfully helped him. The laughter of little Gertrude—her father's "sunshine"—filled the house. He continued to fulfill his love of nature by collecting chickens, pigeons, cats, and dogs. He even amused himself by keeping a beehouse. Moreover, during his first year of practice in Rakwitz, he had earned more than a thousand thalers—a good sum indeed for a young doctor.

The year 1869 passed. So did an epidemic of croup that Koch helped battle in the town. Then came the year 1870. The gathering shadow of war hung heavily over western Europe. Alarming rumors raced swiftly about Rakwitz as spring approached.

In mid-July the Franco-Prussian War broke out. Bismarck had deliberately goaded the aggressive French government into declaring war on Prussia, which was joined by the other German states in the conflict. Highly trained German troops massed on the French border. Under General von Moltke, they won a smashing victory at Sedan on September 1.

All over Germany men were rushing to join the colors. Koch's younger brothers, Hugo, Albert, and Ernst, were soon in France themselves. Robert himself burned to go; after all, one of his old dreams had been that of becoming an army doctor.

Despite his nearsightedness, Koch presented himself at the recruiting office as a volunteer surgeon and was accepted. He was greatly disappointed, however, when he was not sent directly to the front. Instead, he was assigned to a field hospital of the 10th Army Corps, and was just in time to see the effects of the attack on the French town of St. Privat.

Whatever romantic ideas of war Koch may have had, he now forgot them in a hurry. Casualties poured back from the front by the hundreds. It seemed that the whole countryside had been transformed into a gigantic place of misery.

The wounded and dying lay everywhere. Pitiful moans and cries filled the air. Koch felt one great emotion pounding through him as he tended the men—the pride and satisfaction of being able to serve them as a doctor.

In December, he was transferred as chief medical officer of the military hospital at Neuf-Château. Here he treated hundreds of soldiers for typhoid fever. It was in this post that Koch gained experience which was very valuable to him in later life.

"I shall never regret," he wrote home, "that I took this step and served in the war. Quite apart from the scientific knowledge I have gained—much more indeed than I would have had in spending a half year in some clinic—I have also gained much experience of life. This will serve me well in the coming years."

Nor did Koch forget his three younger brothers. He visited them whenever he could, often at the front, bringing them presents and news from home to lessen their

Koch treating German wounded in the Franco-Prussian War.

hardships. In their letters home, they reported that Robert was keeping a "fatherly" eye on them.

By the sixth month of the war, Paris had not yet fallen to its German besiegers. But for Robert Koch the war was over.

The town of Rakwitz wanted its beloved "Herr Doktor" back. His patients were clamoring for him. Application had been made to the army authorities, and the request was granted. Koch left his post as chief medical officer of the 2nd Army Corps and set out for Rakwitz—by way of Clausthal.

Koch greeted his mother warmly. Of the four sons she had in the war, Robert was the only one she was to see return from it. Mathilde Koch did not see the others for she died suddenly in April of 1871, before they returned home.

Meanwhile, Rakwitz had its doctor back once again. He was given a hero's welcome and was now busier than ever with his growing practice. Before long, however, Koch became restless; he had never wanted to live out his life as an ordinary country doctor. A higher position was that of District Physician for the whole area around Wollstein, a small Posen town near Rakwitz. Koch took the necessary examinations and passed them; then he applied for the job.

The appointment was not long in coming. Koch's reputation had spread throughout the countryside and in February of 1872, a letter came from Baron von Unruhe-Bomst, a high District official, offering him the District Physicianship for Wollstein. Koch, of course, accepted it. The post carried with it a yearly salary and, in addition, Koch would be allowed to treat private patients. Before he could be appointed, however, there was a stiff oral examination he would have to take.

In March, Koch successfully passed this test and soon after was officially named District Physician of Wollstein. There he moved with his family in August.

SEVEN

District Physician
of Wollstein

ROBERT KOCH was to spend eight years in the town of Wollstein. They were to be important years, for now he was beginning his serious work in the new science of bacteriology. Moreover, it was to be alone and without adequate equipment that he would make bacteriology a full-fledged science and his own name famous.

These were also contented years for the young doctor and his family, especially for his little daughter who later recalled them as "one long Sunday." Koch had rented a comfortable house, of which Gertrude wrote in later years:

"Four big rooms and a little study was more than enough for us. The large dining room had a wide bay window with an excellent view in three directions. Our long, roomy hall served as a waiting room for father's patients, and led into his office, which had two windows. Father's office was in the back of the house and had plenty of light and sun. Midway between the entrance door and the windows stood his desk; it was always piled high with books and papers."

As in Rakwitz, Koch proved to be a good doctor and his

patients quickly grew to like and respect him. Now, for the first time in his life, he had enough money to live comfortably. In the rear of the house that he had rented was a large garden where he loved to hear the delighted cries of Gertrude at play. There, too, he could play with his daughter, stroll with his wife, or simply sit with the pipe that he loved to smoke.

Koch also kept a veritable zoo in this garden. There were guinea pigs, monkeys, white mice, pigeons, dogs, cats, even foxes. Most of these creatures the young doctor kept for his experiments; others he kept simply because he loved wild life. Koch also became adept at imitating all of them for the benefit of little Gertrude.

Twenty-eight years old at this time, Koch was indeed a happy man. Yet, being the District Physician of Wollstein was also a job that demanded much time and hard work. It meant taking long rides over rough country roads, often in the middle of the night and in the dead of winter, to see his patients. As he rode about in his heavy carriage to attend a sick baby or an ailing farmer, it seemed to the young doctor that the chances of ever seeing the strange animals, plants, and stones of foreign lands were now fewer than ever.

Indeed, as the years passed, Koch found himself settling into exactly the life he had least wished for—that of a typical country doctor. By day and by night, he had to take care of a staggering number of people—people who were in the poorest of circumstances. He was also out of touch with university affairs which he loved and was, in fact, outside the general circle of intellectual activity altogether. More and more, he seemed rooted to the impoverished half-German, half-Polish province where not only his patients, but his family too, needed him.

How was it, then, that Robert Koch did not lapse into the conventionally easy, uncomplicated life of a respected country physician? We do not know for sure, but there may have been several explanations. Possibly it was the same youthful curiosity that led him to collect and dissect plants and animals which now spurred him on to greater work in medicine. Possibly it was the inspiration with which he had been surrounded at Göttingen, notably that of his great teacher Jacob Henle.

At any rate, it was *something* that kept Robert Koch from remaining an ordinary country doctor. Despite the exacting duties of his practice, he snatched every spare hour he could to look through his microscope, to keep his fingers busy with slides and glass covering slips.

Koch had not been at Wollstein long when he felt the need of having a completely private place to work. This he talked over with Emmy, and the two decided that the best place would be Robert's consultation office.

Years later Gertrude Koch recalled how her father's famous makeshift laboratory was set up. "My mother divided the large room in two with a brown curtain suspended on a long pole. The smaller half in the rear was fitted up as a workroom. This was my father's first laboratory, in which he could work more or less undisturbed. At the window was his equipment for making microphotographs, and he hired a carpenter to build the necessary dark room. It stood there like a big closet with a black curtain hanging in front of it. . . . Next to the dark room was an incubator . . . On the opposite side of the room

Dr. Koch often had to ride long distances over country roads to see his patients.

was a small table laden with photographic apparatus, a microscope, and covered glass containers. In each of these sat a white mouse, ready to be used for some experiment."

Koch allowed no one but his wife and child to enter his laboratory, lest some experiment be disturbed. Emmy also had a special duty to perform when her husband was making photographs of some specimen or other. Koch needed sunlight to expose his plates to, but could not always tell when the sun would come out on a cloudy day. Thus Emmy would have to watch the clouds outside the house and yell to Robert inside when they would part and the sun come out again. For this, Emmy earned the nickname of "cloud pusher."

Months before, Emmy had also helped her husband greatly in another way. Knowing that Robert's great wish was someday to own a good microscope, she saved and budgeted in little ways until she had an old beer stein nearly brimful of coins. Koch was overjoyed when his wife presented him with a fine, new Hartnack microscope.

Meanwhile, as Koch was busily snatching minutes from his practice to pour over his microscope, great events were taking place in the scientific world. Over in Paris, Louis Pasteur was exciting medical men with his experiments to prove that communicable diseases are caused by particular living organisms. As a result of Pasteur's work, Joseph Lister in Scotland was demonstrating that a surgical wound could heal without becoming infected—if the dressing used and the hands and instruments of the operating surgeon were kept entirely free from living germs. He was also saving women in childbirth by keeping germs away from them.

Even in faraway Wollstein, Koch had heard of these scientific feats. They were feats which especially interested Koch, since they were connected with the microscope.

The more he heard of the achievements of these men, the more Koch himself longed to share in them. True, his part might be a small and insignificant one, but nevertheless his findings might possibly aid in answering the riddle that was then puzzling the scientific brains of Europe. The riddle was this: Were tiny living beings, too small to be seen with the naked eye, the cause of communicable disease in animals and men—or were they not?

Koch knew it was only on the other side of the brown curtain in his consultation room that he would find out. As time went on, he began leading a kind of "double life."

Outside the brown curtain, Koch was the beloved District Physician; he dealt faithfully and thoughtfully with itches and aches, ringworms and whooping coughs, teethings and infections, births and deaths. But behind the brown curtain, he devoted every spare minute trying to find out the answers to questions that even an ordinary practice such as his furnished. For now, not only were drops of water from the rain barrel outside, and the feelers of insects going under his new microscope, but also bits of infected matter from his own patients. Also, he was learning the importance of keeping his glass slides shining clean as he shoved his specimens under the reflecting mirror.

Oddly enough, in spite of all this activity, Koch also found the time to pursue another scientific interest. Although the fact is little known, he was deeply interested in anthropology. In the country surrounding Wollstein there were remains of ancient villages—strange villages in which the inhabitants had built houses on stilts over marshes and swamps. These sites were then being investigated by authorities from Berlin.

One of these authorities was none other than the famous pathologist, Rudolf Virchow—the same Virchow whose lectures Koch had strained to hear in the Charity Hospital in Berlin. Virchow had interested himself in the bones found in the ancient villages, and in May, 1876, came to the Wollstein countryside to inspect them. Koch, who was also much interested in these sites, went along with Virchow's party to see them.

In renewing their acquaintance, the two men doubtless discussed the progress of medicine. Little did the great Virchow suspect, however, that he and the young country doctor by his side were soon to become intellectual enemies. For, in the near future, he would stand on one side of a medical controversy and Koch on the other.

Nevertheless, it was Koch's constant investigations on the other side of the brown curtain that were dominating his attention now.

This was the year 1876. Koch had recently made a great discovery.

EIGHT

Anthrax!

―――――――――――――――――――――――――――――

LATE one winter afternoon in 1876, Dr. Robert Koch had just finished with a patient in his consultation room. The man, who had just had a painful tooth pulled by the District Physician, left Koch's office clutching his jaw. Koch sighed wearily as he saw four other sick people waiting in his anteroom.

The District Physician was just about to signal for the next patient when a wild-eyed, big-boned Prussian farmer burst into the anteroom. He muttered his apologies, pressed past the waiting patients, and blurted out what—to Koch—had become a familiar story.

"Excuse the interruption, Herr Doktor," muttered the farmer. "I had to come immediately. It's my sheep, you see. My three fine sheep. This morning they were perfectly healthy. I fed them myself out of the same trough. Now one is dead, the other is dying, and—I don't understand it —the third is still in good health. It must be the *Wutkrank-heit*—the raging sickness!"

"*Anthrax* again," nodded Koch, using the medical name for the disease. "Well, let us go and have a look at them."

Koch had left the anteroom door open and the other patients had heard. Some had been waiting over an hour.

Now, as Koch hurried past them throwing on his coat, they began to mutter. Here was their doctor again—rushing off to look at some ailing animal while his human patients could wait for his services.

When Koch arrived at the farmer's barn, he saw just what he had expected to see. There was the healthy sheep eating contentedly away at the common trough. Another sheep stood pathetically in a corner; it refused to eat, its head drooped dejectedly, its eyes shone glassily. A third sheep lay stiff and cold on the barn floor, its uppermost legs stretched out stiff in death.

"Please, Herr Doktor," pleaded the farmer, "can you save the others?"

"No," replied Koch simply. "The one in the corner is dying as you see. The third will probably be dead by morning."

Why then had Koch come? To gaze at dead sheep when he should have been attending to people? Perhaps the same question crossed the unlucky farmer's mind as he saw the District Physician kneel down beside the dead sheep.

Koch had brought with him a clean, carefully stoppered test tube. Into this he drew off some blood from the sheep that had died of anthrax. It was not the deep crimson of healthy blood, but a ghastly blackish color.

Guarding the test tube carefully, Koch returned home. By this time, his disgruntled patients had left. Emmy, who had been seeing less and less of her husband these past months, had gone to bed. She had left some supper for Robert on his worktable, but now it was cold. Koch hardly gave it a glance. Instead, he sat down before his microscope. Between two slides of shining glass, he put a drop or two of the diseased sheep's blood and slid the specimen under the instrument.

There they were again! Floating about in globules of blood were the strange, tiny things that looked like little sticks. Some were very short in the shape of rods; others looked as though they had been hitched together to form long threads.

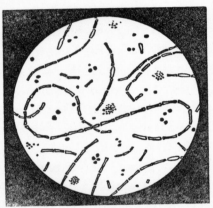

Anthrax bacilli from the blood, as seen through a microscope. Drawing also shows spores.

These quivering little rods and threads were just what Koch had known he *would* see in the diseased animal's blood. For months now he had been examining just such specimens. And in every diseased sample the sinister little sticks and threads seemed to be present.

Moreover, try as he would, Koch had been unable to find them in the blood of healthy animals. The more Koch gazed at the deadly little rods and threads, the more convinced he became that they were the cause of the disease called anthrax.

For decades, anthrax had left a bloody trail across Europe. It could cut down a wealthy farmer's flock of five hundred cattle as swiftly as it could a handful of a poor farmer's. This was the most terrifying thing about the disease: it always struck without the slightest warning. And the countryside around Wollstein, especially, was very susceptible to anthrax attacks—not only to herds of cattle and flocks of sheep, but also occasionally to men.

As in the case of the farmer's sheep that Koch had just seen, a calf might be perfectly well one day, frisking about at its mother's side and eating its food with great appetite. The next day the owner would tell how it would suddenly refuse to eat; how the animal's head and body would droop like a wilted flower; and finally how, before he realized what was wrong with the creature, it would be lying cold and stiff, its blood turned the terrible black color. Then, as likely as not, the farmer would report that the rest of the flock had swiftly become infected and had died in the same violent way. Often, too, the owner himself or a helper would be struck down by anthrax. Large boils would rise on the skin and the victim would die in a fit of terrible coughing.

There seemed to be no way to halt the deadly march of anthrax across the continent of Europe. A mysterious power seemed to be at work, which man could not hope to stop until it had run its course.

Certain research, however, had been carried out before Koch became interested in the disease. In 1845, the French physician Casimir-Joseph Davaine had noticed the curious rods and threads floating about in the blood of anthrax-ridden cattle. Davaine, however, had not identified them with the disease itself. By 1861 a number of other men—notably Rayer in France, and Pollender in Germany—had also noticed the swirling little rods.

In addition, the great microbe-hunting trailblazer, Louis Pasteur, had been investigating this and other diseases caused by bacteria in Paris. "Every disease," Pasteur declared, "is caused by a tiny living germ." Yet, neither Pasteur nor any of these other men had been able to offer proof.

So far, however, all of this preliminary work on anthrax was of little help to the farmers hardest hit by the disease. Unless it were stamped out—and soon—they would be ruined. The very food supply of Europe was now threatened by anthrax.

Toward the end of 1875 and the beginning of 1876, Koch, the unknown country doctor, was becoming more and more absorbed by the problem. He neglected both his practice and his family in order to steal additional time to study the swirling colonies of rods and threads under his microscope.

Now, just as he had needed to study diseased animal blood, he also needed to study the blood of healthy animals. Koch grew to be a familiar sight in the meat shops and slaughterhouses of Wollstein. In time, it was no longer necessary for the District Physician to ask for blood samples from the animals—the butchers, dealers and warehousemen simply nodded that he could take them.

These blood samples that Koch took ran into the hundreds; each regularly went onto the glass slides under his microscope. Day after day and night after night, Koch peered patiently at the healthy samples—then, again, at diseased samples—until he would rise bleary-eyed from the instrument.

A number of questions were now uppermost in Koch's mind:

"Perhaps Pasteur is right," he mused. "Perhaps every disease *is* caused by a germ. But who is to say that these deadly little rods and threads in the diseased blood are truly *alive?* And if they are the real cause of anthrax, how can I prove it *unless* I prove they are alive? To do this, I must actually see them growing, breeding, multiplying . . ."

To really *grow* the disease-causing microbe—that was Koch's task. It was a big order and the District Physician knew it. The winter of 1876 wore on. As Koch racked his brains, a plan began to form in his mind.

NINE

White Mice and a "Hanging Drop"

K OCH soon began to realize that he could not go on experimenting with cattle and sheep alone— whether they were diseased or healthy. The animals were too expensive to buy himself and they were also clumsy to handle. However, he had plenty of white mice scampering around their cages in his laboratory.

"Why not give the disease to them?" Koch asked himself. "Perhaps in these little creatures I can see how the killer grows and multiplies."

In deciding on this approach, Koch got started on the famous set of experiments that were to prove that anthrax bacilli were indeed living organisms.

Koch selected one of his white mice—a particularly healthy specimen—and tried to give it the disease. He failed at first, for he had no syringe with which to inject the diseased material into the mouse's body. The District Physician destroyed several mice before he hit on a way to make an effective injection.

In time, Koch found that simple wooden slivers worked the best. These he carefully cleaned and passed through a flame in an oven to kill any stray bacteria that may have been present on them. Koch would then make a tiny cut at the root of a mouse's tail, dip the sterilized wooden sliver into a drop of diseased black blood and scrape some of it off into the cut.

Using this technique, Koch finally inoculated his first mouse successfully. Into the tiny cut in the mouse's tail had gone a bit of blackish blood from a sheep dead of anthrax.

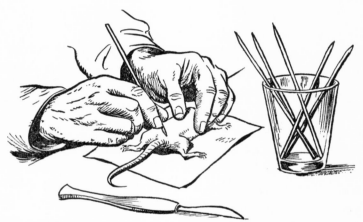

Koch using wooden slivers to inoculate white mice.

The physician then dropped the mouse into a separate cage. He spent the rest of that day taking care of patients; then he went to bed wondering what he would see in the cage next day.

In the morning, Koch awoke, went to his laboratory, and parted the brown curtain. There in the cage, as Koch had hoped, the mouse lay dead, its feet poking stiffly up in the air, its fur no longer sleek and white, but turned a dirty gray.

Immediately the District Physician pinned the pitiful animal down to his table and began dissecting it. Inside he found the mouse's spleen incredibly black and swollen. Koch took a bit of the diseased matter and slid it under his microscope.

As he looked excitedly, Koch knew that he had transferred to the mouse the dreaded disease that had killed the sheep only hours before. It was the same disease that went by a dozen names—the *Rotz,* the *Wutkrankheit, Milzbrand*—anthrax. There, swarming under the lens of his microscope, were the familiar rods and threads.

For the next month, the District Physician could not tear himself away from his laboratory and his cages of white mice. Beginning with the first dead mouse, Koch now took another healthy mouse, made the tiny cut in its tail, and injected a little black blood from the first victim.

In twenty-four hours, this mouse too was dead. From the second victim, Koch inoculated a third. When that one was dead, he scraped a bit of its blackish blood into the tail of a fourth. Koch repeated this procedure some thirty times, always with the same result. Each time he would inject a healthy mouse with the blood from a mouse that had just died of anthrax—and each time the new mouse would die.

There was one trouble, however. His experiments only proved that he could transfer the disease from one animal to another. He still had no conclusive proof that the rods and threads were alive, for he had never really seen them *grow*.

A less cautious man than Koch would simply have *assumed* that the deadly little microbes grew amazingly fast, choking the bodies of the mice until they died. After all, the drop of blood on each wooden sliver, with which he inoculated each mouse, contained perhaps only a few hundred rods and threads. Obviously, when the disease spread through the body of the mouse, their number had to increase by the *billions*. Even when he looked at a sample through his microscope there were as many as twenty-five thousand to the inch!

The persistent country doctor was far from satisfied.

"I *must* see the rods actually growing," Koch muttered. "I must find a way to grow them myself *outside the body of an animal*. There must be some way to nourish and feed them. But I must be careful not to kill or damage them either. Just holding them fast would do it—then I could watch them grow."

But how? Koch tried everything he could think of and failed time and again. He correctly reasoned that, if he were to succeed, he must duplicate the material and conditions of an animal's body itself. He tried growing diseased mouse spleen in the watery liquid from an ox's eye, then keeping it at the temperature of a mouse's body in his homemade incubator. These little solutions he would try to keep between glass slides, but always—just as he thought he could see the rods growing—other microbes would steal in and spoil the experiment.

Frustrated, but with his mind still on the problem, Koch would emerge from his laboratory to deliver some peasant woman's baby or treat a child's croupy cough. The people of Wollstein had noticed how absent-minded and short-tempered their doctor was growing. Word had gotten around that Herr Doktor Koch was searching for tiny bugs that he said were capable of killing whole herds of cattle.

"Dr. Koch says it is these very bugs that are causing the 'raging sickness,' " the villagers whispered. "Surely this is nonsense. How can he waste his time like this?"

Koch completely ignored this village gossip. By spring he had thought of a way to pin down the anthrax microbes so he could watch them grow.

It was a simple but ingenious device. Koch took a fairly thick glass slide and gouged out a small well in it. Next, he took a thin glass slide and heated it to destroy any existing microbes that might be on it. On this thin slide, he placed a drop of the watery liquid from the eye of an ox. Into this drop, he slid a bit of spleen from a mouse that had just died of anthrax. Then, taking the thicker slide in which he had gouged out the well, he sealed off the drop by placing that slide over the thin one. To make sure the drop was securely imprisoned, Koch spread a little petroleum jelly around the well so that the two slides stuck firmly together.

Now, when Koch turned this device upside down, he had a perfect "hanging drop" protected from all other microbes except those of anthrax. In addition, the entire thing was made of glass so that Koch could easily watch what might happen inside.

Koch then placed the arrangement under his microscope and waited for results. Nothing happened for nearly two hours. Suddenly, as he watched the tiny pieces of infected spleen through the lens, a few of the little sticks began to divide and grow! Then these, too, would break in half and lengthen. After some hours, Koch's whole drop-specimen was filled with long threads tangled together in complete confusion. Now even the hard-to-convince Koch was certain that the rods were alive, for he himself had seen them grow.

Koch's "hanging drop" device.

Tough-minded doctor though he was, the sight of these multiplying microscopic murderers made the District Physician's flesh crawl. Here he was seeing anthrax in action. Just as these creatures were multiplying by the millions before his very eyes, so they as swiftly spread through the body of a strong ox or bull, clogging the creature's arteries until it was dead in a few short hours.

Koch knew what his next step had to be. From the deadly specimen he had just grown, he transplanted a bit to another hanging drop. The same thing happened a second time. From the few isolated rods, countless other rods and threads quickly spread and choked the drop.

Eight times Koch repeated this experiment. Finally, in the eighth hanging drop, there remained none of the original mouse's tissue. What the physician now had were only the descendants of those bacilli that had killed the mouse a few days before.

Could these, too, commit murder? To Koch, this was the

most important question of all. Excitedly, he made a small cut in a healthy mouse's tail and with a wooden splinter transferred a bit of the eighth drop.

"Now we shall see," breathed Koch with a nervous sigh. "I have grown these bacilli pure and to the eighth generation away from other microbes. If they are really the cause of anthrax, the mouse cannot live."

Twenty-four hours later the mouse was dead! Koch quickly dissected the creature and looked at a bit of its spleen under the microscope. There again were the familiar twisted masses of rods and threads.

Even now the hard-to-convince country doctor was not satisfied. He grew more pure generations of anthrax bacilli in more hanging drops. This time he injected the deadly fluid into a dozen other animals—sheep, guinea pigs, rabbits, cats. Each time the result was the same—the creatures died horribly as the fatal blackness clogged their blood and tissues.

Koch was now as sure as he would ever be of the truth: the swirling little rods were without doubt the villains in the tragedy of anthrax. Moreover, the evidence seemed just about conclusive for the first of Koch's great contributions to medical science; namely, the fact that only one kind of microbe can cause one kind of disease.

Alone, using crude homemade equipment, forced to invent his own methods of investigation, Koch had accomplished a major medical achievement.

Meanwhile, however, one piece of the anthrax jigsaw puzzle was still missing. Koch knew he would have to track it down if the whole terrible history of anthrax bacilli were to be completely clear.

Koch Solves the Final Mystery of Anthrax

As SAVAGE and deadly as Koch knew the swarming little rods and threads of anthrax could be, he had noticed something strangely fragile about them. It seemed that, under certain conditions, they could perish and fade away as quickly as they could multiply and kill!

More than once the District Physician had smeared one of his glass slides with a bit of diseased anthrax tissue only to see the bacilli break up, shrink, and finally disappear before his very eyes. Even when he tried to nourish them with one of their favorite foods—the watery liquid from an ox's eye—they sometimes refused to grow. On another occasion, he had noticed that if the anthrax bacilli were exposed to the rays of the sun they soon perished.

Koch was greatly puzzled; but of one thing he was sure: the deadly bacilli did not seem to live long outside a nourishing substance.

"How is it then," Koch asked himself, "that they obviously *do* survive from one winter to the next in pastures where cattle and sheep die year after year? If these bacteria are so delicate, how can they remain alive in the open air of these fields all year round?"

Aside from the damage anthrax was doing around Wollstein, Koch knew that conditions were much worse in other parts of Europe. In central France, for example, there were dangerous mountain pastures and deadly green meadows where few farm animals could feed without dying of anthrax. No matter how fertile these fields seemed to be, no matter how fat the cattle grew, whole herds seemed to perish almost overnight. The farmers and peasants of these regions were sure that their fields were cursed. Superstitions of all kinds were being spread about the disease. A black scourge seemed loose over the land and men were powerless to stop it.

The Wollsteiners, too, were terrified of anthrax. They had also become suspicious of the work Koch was doing. It seemed unthinkable to them that—as Koch was claiming—a tiny creature only a twenty-thousandth of an inch long was the murderer of their flocks. They, too, had become greatly puzzled as to why this killer was rampant in one place and not in another.

"If these little bugs of yours are really killing our cattle, Herr Doktor," they said, "how is it that they are not in every field? In one meadow the cows remain healthy and fat, in another they die like rats."

How and why indeed? Koch only wished he had the answer. So the disease appeared in one area and not another. And somehow it lived on year after year—in the cold, the open air, even in sunlight—to strike again and again. The problem was really the same in all these questions: how did the disease *transmit* itself?

The dogged District Physician was to find the answer quicker than he thought.

One day, as he was examining one of his hanging drop specimens under the microscope, Koch saw something strange happen. This specimen he had kept warm—at the temperature of a mouse's body—for twenty-four hours. By all rights, the drop should now be swarming with the twisted threads of anthrax bacilli.

Koch noticed immediately that it was not! At least, they were not the kind of threads he had expected to see.

What Koch saw instead were tiny oval bodies like pearl beads strung along one after another. In fact, they resembled miniature pearl necklaces under his lens.

The first thing that occurred to the country doctor was that other microbes had somehow gotten into the hanging drop and spoiled the pure growth of the anthrax bacilli. He took another long and careful look.

"No," he muttered, "that cannot be either. I see now that the little pearls are *inside* what ought to be the usual threads. This can only mean that the bacilli have transformed themselves into the pearls!"

Koch shrugged, dried the hanging drop, and put the peculiar specimen away for a few weeks. Then he proceeded to forget all about it. Purely by chance one day, he picked it up again and slid it under his lens. There—as before—shone the same tiny pearl-like beads!

Then Koch made one of the most fortunate moves of his career. He decided to see what would happen if, once again, he covered it with the pure fluid from an ox's eye. Onto the dried-up, weeks'-old smear the liquid went.

Koch was now dumbfounded at what he saw.

The pearl-like beads were actually sprouting and growing again! Back they turned again into the familiar
swarming, twisting rods and threads of active anthrax
bacilli. It was as if they had only been sleeping these many
weeks.

This same idea of "sleeping" bacilli passed through
Koch's mind. Now he thought he knew what had happened.

"I see it!" he said aloud, his words muffled by the drawn
brown curtain. "These pearl-like things must be the tough
form of the microbe—the *spores.* No wonder they can
live in the open air and through the winter! In this form,
they could easily survive in cold, hot, or dry weather."

If he was right, Koch reasoned further, this phenomenon
also explained how the disease could be transmitted year
after year. The cattle grazing in the meadows swallowed
the spores, which later grew back again into the fatal
killers that took the lives of the animals.

Later research proved that Koch's guess was absolutely
right. Today, we know that the class of bacilli of which
anthrax is a member can shrink into little round balls.
These little balls, called *spores,* build up strong walls to
shield them against warmth, dryness, sunlight, and harmful chemicals. In this way, the bacilli stay alive for long
periods of time, even without food and water. When living conditions improve, the walls burst and the bacilli
push out again. In Koch's case, these conditions improved
when he provided the nourishing watery liquid from the
ox's eye.

As usual, however, Koch refused to be convinced by
one experiment. If his guess about the life history of an-

thrax was correct, he would have to prove it by more experiments. He took several more specimens of diseased mouse spleens and kept them at the temperature of a mouse's body for twenty-four hours. Once again, the bacilli shrank into the hard, round, pearl-like spores.

And again Koch got them to hatch out into active bacilli when he smeared them with the fluid from an ox's eye. Then he tried inoculating his white mice with the spores. The blood-food of the mice, of course, improved living conditions for the spores enormously. The spores then hatched into active anthrax bacilli, and the mice died.

Through these and other experiments, the truth now became clear to Koch: the *spores,* not the bacilli themselves, were the transmitters of anthrax.

Koch also found that anthrax bacilli never formed into spores in the body of a live animal. The animal had to be dead and, moreover, it had to be kept quite warm. To prove this, Koch kept some anthrax bacilli on ice for a week; no spores were able to form and the specimens were quite harmless.

Koch now knew what advice he could give the hard-pressed cattle and sheep growers: If possible, burn the bodies of all creatures dead of anthrax; if that is not possible, bury them deep in the earth where the cold will prevent the bacilli from going into the spore state. In this way, you may stamp out anthrax.

Never, up to this time, had a scientist seen the complete life history of a microbe unfold before his eyes. It was by persistent hard work, originality, and patience that Koch had managed to witness this scientific spectacle. He felt excited. His experiments told him that he was right. Now he badly wanted to tell someone of his discoveries—someone of unquestioned medical authority.

It was on this April evening in the year 1876 that Dr. Robert Koch sat down and wrote his all-important letter to Dr. Ferdinand Cohn of the Botanical Institute in Breslau.

ELEVEN

Europe Learns of Dr. Koch

THIRTY-TWO-YEAR-OLD Dr. Robert Koch waited nervously in the Wollstein station for the train to Breslau that April morning. Dressed in his best suit, he kept peering nearsightedly down the track through his gold-rimmed spectacles. The train was already late.

When it finally ground to a stop in the station, Koch picked up a suitcase in one hand and a partly covered cage in the other, and boarded a third-class coach. In the cage were a few dozen squealing white mice. Packed away in the suitcase was Koch's microscope and several hanging drops of deadly anthrax bacilli.

Dr. Koch, the unknown country doctor, was on his way to demonstrate to the experts in Breslau the life history of the anthrax bacillus.

The elderly Dr. Cohn had been waiting for Koch's visit to the Botanical Institute. On April 30, 1876, Cohn gathered together a number of brilliant men to witness the District Physician's demonstration. Among these were Leopold Auerbach, the physiologist; and Julius Cohnheim, the noted pathologist. Also present was Karl Weigert, who had been the first to stain cultures with dyes so that their development could be watched accurately.

Standing before these famous medical men, Koch's words came haltingly at first, nervously. Soon, however, he was speaking surely and confidently as he went from step to step in the experiments that had taken him years to work out successfully.

Koch's demonstration lasted for three days.

As they watched, the brilliant doctors looked at Koch with more and more respect. He handled his microscope and slides like a veteran scientist. The man seemed incredibly sure of himself.

Slowly the facts about anthrax unrolled under the bright mirror of Koch's microscope. By the end of his three-day demonstration, Koch had cultivated before these men the anthrax bacilli in pure cultures, dyed them with Weigert's dyes, and shown how they developed from spores in the liquid from the eye of an ox; he had also grown them into long chains and injected them into his white mice.

As if he had not shown them enough, Koch repeatedly demonstrated that the deadly bacilli were constantly present in the contagious material; again and again, he isolated them from it and proved their killing power on his little animals. In this way, patiently and without excitement, Robert Koch traced for his audience the life cycle of anthrax. He had also given them the first clear evidence that a microscopically tiny organism was the cause of an infectious disease.

Koch's audience was delighted with this masterly presentation. Julius Cohnheim became so excited that he rushed out of the room and over to his own laboratory where his students were working.

"Drop whatever you are doing and go at once to Koch!" Professor Cohnheim gasped to them. "This man has made a splendid discovery."

"But Herr Professor," one student cut in, "who is this Koch?"

"It does not matter who he is. It is what he has done," snapped Cohnheim. "Koch has produced something absolutely complete. There is nothing more to be done! I consider this the greatest discovery in the field of microorganisms. Mark my words, Koch will astonish and shame us with still further discoveries!"

The students were now pulling on their coats and rushing off to see this unknown man and the results of his work. Among them was a young man named Paul Ehrlich, later to become famous himself in the science of medicine.

Once again Koch emphasized before the whole group the significance of his discovery. "Each disease," he repeated, "is caused by one particular microbe—and by one alone. Only the anthrax microbe causes anthrax; only a typhoid microbe can cause typhoid fever."

One by one, the brilliant men in Koch's audience shook his hand and congratulated him. Cohn and Cohnheim were especially enthusiastic. Both men themselves had previously guessed at the possibility of spores in the life cycle of anthrax, yet they were not jealous of Koch because he had first demonstrated it. Honest and generous scientists, they thought only of trying to help Koch go further in his work. Indeed, it was largely through their enthusiasm that Koch's name began to become known throughout Europe.

"My dear Koch," said Julius Cohnheim, "what you must

do next is clear. You must go and submit your findings to Virchow himself."

Recognizing that Rudolf Virchow was the greatest name in German medical science, Koch agreed to go to Berlin and see him. When he arrived, however, Koch found the great physician cool and distant. Nothing that the country doctor said or demonstrated seemed to interest Virchow in the least. Finally, Koch left his office, bitter and disappointed at how Virchow had received him.

These two great men never managed to understand one another. And because Virchow currently dominated German medicine, Koch, from this time on, determined to avoid him.

The District Physician now returned to his country practice in Wollstein. There his brown-curtained laboratory waited for him. Not only was there much for him to do in it, but Koch had now made up his mind to publish his findings. He first broke his silence of many years by writing a forty-page article that appeared in Dr. Cohn's *Contributions to the Biology of Plants.* In it Koch described his recent work on anthrax; the article now stands as a classic of medical history.

Other publications quickly followed. About a year after his dramatic presentation in Breslau, Koch wrote a paper describing his methods of studying microbes. He explained how he placed the microbe-laden material on a glass cover-slip, and how he stained the microbes with dyes so that they stood out and could be recognized in the tissues where they were present.

In the summer of 1877, Koch made frequent trips to Dr. Cohnheim's laboratory in Breslau. The two men had grown fond of each other and, in experimenting together, Koch began to stress the importance of photographing their results. Up to this time, scientists had had to depend on word-descriptions and sketches of what they saw through their microscopes. This naturally created much confusion because no two descriptions of sketches were exactly alike. As Koch himself later expressed the situation: "The literature on bacteria had been allowed to swell into a muddy stream."

As a result, Koch also published a paper describing his techniques in "fixing" microbes so that they could be photographed. For this purpose he used Weigert's methods of staining so that the tiny microbes in tissues would clearly stand out. By further use of special condensers, diaphragms, and lenses placed in oil, Koch pioneered the techniques of *microphotography* that are still in use today.

The following year, in 1878, Koch wrote another paper describing an important investigation he had made in regard to wound infections. About this time, he also spoke out against other scientists who were claiming that microbes could change types—one into another. Again Koch emphasized that such a belief was nonsense: every microbe had its own certain shape, size, and special growing conditions.

Toward the close of the decade, Koch's work was growing more and more complicated. Hampered by his crude equipment, cramped into his little laboratory, he began to long for a larger, well-equipped place to work.

Meanwhile Koch's friends, Cohn and Cohnheim, had not forgotten him. In fact, they had been constantly working in his interest, praising his work everywhere. Germany should be ashamed, they said, to have such a distinguished scientist hidden away in a little country town. Such a man ought to be in a city near other scientists where he could give his full time to the study of microbes.

At last, Cohn and Cohnheim succeeded in having Koch appointed City Physician in Breslau. This position would pay him double what he received in Wollstein. Koch accepted it and moved there with his family in 1879.

He was to remain in Breslau only three months, however. Living in the city proved more expensive than Koch had bargained for. Moreover, there were so many other doctors in the neighborhood that he could obtain very few private patients. Worse still, he seemed to have even less time for his scientific studies. Early in 1880, he was back in Wollstein again, much to the delight of the Wollsteiners who respected and trusted him.

But the world had begun to take notice of Robert Koch's name and his work. He would not have to spend very many more weeks in his little backwoods laboratory. In the spring of 1880, the German government appointed him an associate of the Imperial Health Office in Berlin.

This was to be the last time Koch would change addresses. Though he visited many countries in later years, it was always to the German capital city that he returned.

TWELVE

Koch Finds a New Way to Grow Microbes

I N July of 1880, Robert Koch reported for work at the Imperial Health Office in Berlin. For some months now, progress in bacteriology had been slow there and Koch was immediately provided with everything he needed to begin his researches.

Here Koch found himself in a fine, well-equipped laboratory where he could devote full time to the study of microbes. If he needed special apparatus, there was always plenty of money to buy it. In addition, Koch was assigned two brilliant, young military doctors as assistants—Friedrich Loeffler and Georg Gaffky.

At first, the former country doctor did not know what to give these young men to do. Until now he had always worked alone, had done everything himself. In the morning, Koch would enter the laboratory, greet his assistants shyly and begin work, leaving Loeffler and Gaffky idle.

Soon, however, Koch realized that the two young physicians were serious scientists like himself. They were hard-working, loyal, conscientious and as eager for original work as he was. In a short time, they were working as a devoted team. Before the three windows of the laboratory, Koch would sit on a stool in the center peering through his microscope, with Loeffler and Gaffky on either side of him.

Koch astonished his assistants almost daily with new discoveries about the world of microbes. Later, other students—some of them from foreign lands—came to work under the brilliant Robert Koch. Indeed, this period has been called the Golden Age of Bacteriology. The science was young, and young men were devoting themselves to it all over the world. But nowhere was more being found out about the microbial world than here in Koch's own laboratory. Koch himself later wrote of this as "a period where the gold lay all on the surface: all one had to do was pick it up."

The first task that Koch and his helpers set themselves was to improve still further the technique of studying microbes.

One problem had been bothering Koch for years. Up till then, no one had been able to invent a simple and sure way of obtaining pure *cultures*—growths—of microbes. This was because the food on which they were grown (called the *culture medium*) was a liquid. Each time a scientist worked with a mixture of microbes in such a liquid, he could only manage to separate one from the other with the greatest difficulty. Yet there seemed no other way to do this if the scientist wanted to grow one kind of microbe for study purposes.

Robert Koch was the first man to hit on a method of growing pure cultures from a mixture of microbes. It was a discovery that many consider to be Koch's greatest contribution to bacteriology. Curiously, it was made by pure accident.

One morning Koch happened to glance at his laboratory table. On it, overnight, had been left a slice of boiled potato. Noticing tiny spots of color on the cut side of the vegetable, he picked it up and looked at it more closely. Nearly every color of the rainbow seemed to be there— one spot was red, another yellow, a third violet. Koch suspected that the little specks were microbes that had fastened themselves onto the potato from the air and were now growing. But why were they different colors?

With a bit of thin platinum wire, Koch transferred some of the material from one of the specks onto a glass slide and put it under his microscope. As he suspected, Koch saw a mass of bacilli swarming about in the specimen. But there was one thing about them that made Koch gasp.

They were all alike! Each bacillus was exactly like its thousands of companions. Koch now excitedly examined other droplets on the boiled potato. Again the same result! Each of the droplets was made up of microbes of the same kind. Some were rodlike sticks, others were corkscrew in shape, still others were simply round—but always there was but one kind in each bit of material.

"Loeffler! Gaffky!" cried Koch, calling his assistants. "Take a look at this!"

The young doctors did so. They, too, gasped. "But Herr Doktor," said the mystified Loeffler, "these are pure cultures. How did you get them?"

"Very simply," said Koch. "Nature made them for me overnight on this slice of potato. I believe this is the clue

"I believe this is the clue we have been looking for," said Koch to Loeffler and Gaffky.

we have been looking for. If I am right, we are on the track of a solid culture medium."

Koch went on to explain what he thought had happened, and where they had been making their mistake up to now.

One of the favorite culture mediums of that time was liquid gelatin. No matter how hard scientists tried to grow pure cultures in these mixtures, foreign microbes from the air would fall into them. Inevitably, the result would be a hopeless mixture of different microbes.

"But," objected Koch, "when they fall from the air onto the hard surface of some solid food like this potato, each has to remain where it falls. They cannot swim about as they did in the liquid and get all mixed together. Each microbe has to stay where it settles, then it multiplies and forms a pure colony made up of its own kind and no other."

Koch knew, however, that he would have to back up his guesswork with confirming experiments. He and his assistants set to work. Day after day, using various mixtures of microbes, they painted the sides of bushels of boiled potatoes. The results were just as Koch predicted. Wherever a separate microbe landed, there it remained and multiplied into a pure colony of its own kind.

Soon, Koch began to realize that using potatoes as solid culture mediums was only a signpost pointing to a much better method of growing pure colonies of microbes. The microbes still seemed to thrive best on the liquid gelatin. Why not—he reasoned—change the proportions of gelatin and water so that the mixture would harden when it cooled?

Koch decided to try this. Into shallow, wide dishes he poured some warm, newly mixed gelatin solution. Then he added some beef broth to provide food for the microbes. When the mixture cooled and became solid, Koch pricked over its surface with a wire that had been dipped into a mixture of germs. Where each microbe came to settle on the surface of the gelatin, there a colony grew!

Robert Koch had at last found a way to separate a mixture of microbes and to grow each in a pure culture of its own breed. Although the method seems quite simple, it was a great achievement—one that helped revolutionize the science of bacteriology. Indeed, from Koch's day to the present, the use of solid culture mediums remains one of the best ways to grow microbes in pure colonies.

Realizing the importance of this new technique, Koch decided to swallow his pride and go again to Dr. Virchow. Surely this time the great physician would listen to his findings and tell other scientists of his approval.

Once again, Virchow was cool and distant to Koch. What the young man claimed about growing pure colonies of microbes so simply seemed impossible. Koch's enthusiasm did not impress the Dean of German Medicine. Virchow was now an old man; he had discovered much. Koch was surely just another of the vast army of microbe hunters who had made a slight advance here or there. Koch, depressed and disappointed, left Virchow, redoubling his decision to completely avoid the man from now on.

THIRTEEN

Koch Attacks Tuberculosis

IT WAS now August of 1881, and the Imperial Health Office sent Robert Koch as one of the German delegates to the International Medical Congress in London.

Here Koch met the most famous medical men of his day. Among them were Louis Pasteur, the great French microbe hunter, and the two famous English surgeons, Lord Joseph Lister and Sir James Paget. Rudolf Virchow was also there, but Koch took pains to keep away from him.

Although Lister, Pasteur, and Virchow—the leading lights of their respective countries—dominated the Congress, Robert Koch now became known in England. In Lister's own laboratory at King's College, Koch demonstrated his new technique for growing pure colonies of microbes.

Despite the fact that Koch had spoken out against some of Pasteur's work a few years earlier, Pasteur generously rushed up to Koch and exclaimed: "This is certainly great progress, Monsieur!" Unfortunately, these two great scientists were to remain opponents the rest of their lives.

Years later, a curious question arose about this same London Medical Congress. Did Robert Koch—at this early date—actually show anyone in London that he had grown a pure culture of tuberculosis?

One report says that he did. And to no less a person than Lord Lister himself! Other reports say that Koch could not have made any such discovery for he had only made his first inoculations of tubercular material on his return from London.

The truth is that probably Koch had talked of the dreaded disease to Lord Lister—and to anyone else who would listen. It was a great deal on his mind. Since his Rakwitz and Wollstein days, he had come to hate this killer of men, women, and children.

When Robert Koch returned to Berlin, he knew he had now perfected the basic tools with which to fight a most vicious disease—tuberculosis.

For hundreds of years, tuberculosis had been the most dreaded of human diseases. During the nineteenth century, over thirty million persons had died of it. In Europe and America alone, the disease regularly claimed the lives of three people out of every seven.

Called "the White Plague," tuberculosis had always been terribly widespread. Over the whole globe, no one was safe from it. Moreover, tuberculosis was seldom detected until it had reached an advanced stage—too late for anyone to do anything about it. There was nothing, in fact, for a tubercular patient to do except prepare for a long and agonizing illness. If by some lucky chance he recovered, no one would believe that he had had tuberculosis in the first place.

As early as the ancient Greeks, tuberculosis had been a common killer. The Greek physicians called the disease *phthisis,* which means "wasting away." Later, the marauder was called "consumption" from the Latin word *consumere*—to consume, or eat away. Both these names arose from the disease's chief symptom; namely, the gradual wasting away of the body. Ancient physicians tried to fight the disease by building up the body through diet, change of climate, and proper exercise and rest. Although this means of combating tuberculosis was quite sensible, it was usually ineffective, for diagnosis of the disease often came so late that the treatment was of no use.

Consumption continued to be as baffling as it was deadly in the centuries that followed. It was not until Koch's own century that medical science began to penetrate the mystery of the disease.

In 1839, a Swiss physician, Dr. J. L. Schoenbein, pointed out that little growths called *tubercles*—knobs or tiny lumps—were often found on the bodies of persons who had died of consumption. Schoenbein then suggested that the disease should be called *tuberculosis.*

But neither Schoenbein nor other medical men of his time could seem to settle one important question about tuberculosis. Was this killer a contagious disease—one that was introduced into the body from outside? Or was it a *constitutional,* or inherited, disease—one that arose of itself in the body, or that was passed on from parents to children? Many medical men, including Virchow, favored the latter view.

"The disease is doubtless inherited," this school stated

gloomily. "If your father had tuberculosis, the chances are good that you will probably get it."

Actually, the one thing that was known about the disease was that it had to be caused by some kind of microbe, for medical researchers had succeeded in transmitting it from infected human beings to healthy animals. A French physician, Jean-Antoine Villimin, had already demonstrated this. So, in fact, had Koch's friend, Julius Cohnheim. He had put a bit of sick tissue from a tubercular patient into the eye of a rabbit and the animal had died of consumption.

Cohnheim's work made many scientists believe—rightly —that the cause of tuberculosis was a living "something." Cohnheim himself predicted that soon someone would find "tubercle particles," as he called them. Encouraged by this, other scientists set out at once to work on the problem of finding these "living somethings." Between the years 1877 and 1881, a whole series of men claimed that they had found the cause of tuberculosis. While it is probable that many of them really did see the tubercle bacillus, they were unable to stain it with dyes or otherwise bring forward enough proof of their discoveries.

Meanwhile, the treatment of those who had the disease had not advanced much either. The only new scheme had been to send tubercular patients to places called *sanitariums*—retreats usually located high in the mountains where they were supposed to get better by sitting outside wrapped in blankets, and breathing in the clear mountain air. However, since the question of whether consumption was catching or not had not been settled, the sanitariums dared not suggest any sanitary regulations concerning tuberculosis. Thus there was no fumigation (disinfecting by gas or smoke), no sterilization, no laws about spitting, and no really advanced means of diagnosing the dreaded disease.

In the summer of 1881, Robert Koch set out on the trail of this "living something"—the tubercle bacillus. Those who knew him well were aware that no subject interested him as much as this dreaded disease.

"Cholera, bubonic plague, and other diseases," Koch once said, "carry off their hundreds, even thousands. But tuberculosis claims its victims in all civilized countries in the *tens* of thousands."

His practice in East Prussia had taught Koch that few families escaped tuberculosis—some member somewhere was always being struck down by it. In fact, Koch was so impressed with the deadliness of tuberculosis that throughout the rest of his life—even to the very end—he let no chance escape to further investigate it.

Moreover, Koch was always very practical in his work. He made it a point always to know where he was going— or at least try to know.

Thus, in beginning his research on tuberculosis, Koch had already worked out in his mind a set of rules as a guide to further experiments with microbes. These four rules, which he later published, have become known as *Koch's Postulates*. They are considered fundamental in bacteriology today:

1. In order to prove that a certain microbe is the cause of a certain disease, that same microbe must be found present in all cases of the disease.

2. This microbe must then be completely separated from the diseased body and grown outside that body in a pure culture.

3. This pure culture must be capable of giving the disease to healthy animals by inoculating them with it.

4. The same microbe should then be obtained from the animals so inoculated, and then grown again in a pure culture outside the body.

If, reasoned Koch, these four conditions could be fulfilled in the case of the tuberculosis microbe, the chain of evidence would be complete. He would then have isolated and grown pure the cause of tuberculosis—the tubercle bacillus.

From the beginning, Koch had to advance step-by-step, inventing new techniques and culture-growing media as he went along.

True, Koch had always been a hard worker and accustomed to many failures. But now he never worked harder —and never did he fail as often. Again, too, he was searching alone, for his two brilliant assistants were tracking down microbes of their own; Gaffky was later to isolate the typhoid bacillus and Loeffler, eventually, that of diphtheria.

Koch had studied Cohnheim's experiments closely; he decided to repeat the experiment of giving tuberculosis to healthy animals. First, he obtained some diseased tissue from the body of a recently dead laborer. A large, powerful man of thirty-five, this victim had entered Berlin's Charity Hospital only days before. As the days went by, the man's cough grew worse; he spat up blood and complained of terrible pains in his chest. Soon his once-superb body had wasted away until he was only a bag of bones. Then the man lay dead, his tissues shot through with the yellowish speckles of tuberculosis.

Koch peered into every part of the unfortunate man's body with his microscope. Day after day passed and he could see nothing more than the dead tissue itself. Nevertheless, he kept inoculating his laboratory animals with the diseased stuff, wondering how long it would take the deadly material to cause their deaths.

While he waited, Koch hurried every morning after breakfast to the Charity Hospital to obtain additional diseased material for his investigations. He inoculated more and more guinea pigs and rabbits with tuberculosis. When they eventually wasted away and died, Koch used their diseased tissues for study. Still, he could not seem to manage to see the killer-bacillus through his microscope.

Two things were now clear to Koch. Unlike the anthrax bacillus, the tubercle bacillus was a very small microbe indeed. Thus, the job of isolating it—even seeing it—would be that much harder. Also, the microbes of tuberculosis were slow growers compared with the fast-multiplying ones of anthrax. Therefore, his attempts to grow them would take far longer.

Still, Koch was sure that the bacilli must be in the tubercles, or tiny lumps, that he found in the tissues of those who had died of tuberculosis. Yet even when he ground them up and looked at them with the best microscopes available in Berlin, he could not see the bacilli. He then tried various methods of dyeing his specimens.

As the days went by, Koch's hands turned nearly every color of the rainbow as he experimented with different dyes. Then they would turn jet black as he dipped them constantly into bichloride of mercury to kill any stray microbes that could have ruined his experiments.

Finally, he found that the dye called methylene blue seemed to be best for his purposes. Now he kept his glass slides for long hours in this blue stain, hoping eventually to see the tubercle bacillus itself.

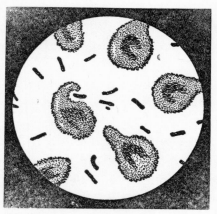

Tubercle bacilli as seen through a microscope.

One day he removed one of his glass slips from this solution and slid it under his microscope. From the tiny chunks of cheesy tubercular matter, a deadly picture emerged for Koch to see. There they were at last—slim, little blue-colored rods—the bacilli of tuberculosis! Far smaller and more curved than those of anthrax, Koch estimated they could not be longer than one fifteen-thousandth of an inch.

The material Koch was examining was a bit of diseased tissue from the dead laborer. He now examined other specimens—from this man—that had also been stained with the blue dye. The same slim little bacilli turned up in each specimen.

"*Nein, nein,*" muttered Koch, "nowhere have I seen these crooked little devils inside the bodies of healthy men or animals."

Koch now turned his attention to the rabbits and guinea pigs he had inoculated with the diseased tissue. They were wasting away and dying in great numbers. He took diseased tissue from them and dipped specimen after specimen in the blue stain. Then they would go under his microscope.

"You see!" he would call to Loeffler and Gaffky. "They are present again. In every case, I find the same crooked little blue-stained sticks."

Still Koch was not satisfied. He had to have even more evidence—evidence that in all cases of tuberculosis these same bacilli would appear. Now he haunted grim morgues and death houses, hospitals and slaughter pens to get more specimens. Later, every hospital in Berlin was directed to send him material from the tissues of people who had died of consumption. From the wasted bodies of these victims, he shot this diseased material into hundreds of healthy animals. And Koch used any and all animals he could lay his hands on—monkeys, dogs, guinea pigs, mice, cats, chickens, even pigeons. Indeed, it was the most relentless and thorough campaign of inoculation that Koch had ever launched.

"—And my results are always the same," announced Koch to the busy Gaffky and Loeffler one day. "One by one, these creatures have all died, and in every specimen taken from them are the same blue-stained rods."

Loeffler and Gaffky congratulated their teacher. Surely this was proof enough that the tubercle bacillus was the cause of tuberculosis. Why not publish? Why not announce his findings to the world?

Koch shook his head. He had, he said, only completed the first step. The next would be to actually grow these slender, crooked rods in a pure culture, outside the body of an animal.

Here again Koch found himself faced with difficulties. He tried growing his bacilli in dozens of test tubes and bottles in dozens of ways. He tried cultivating them on beef broth jelly, in gelatin soups, and at different temperatures. But they would grow on none of the food that Koch prepared for them. They seemed to want to feed only in living bodies.

After many discouraging failures, Koch at last hit on a culture medium that duplicated as nearly as possible the material of which a living body is made. This was his famous blood-serum jelly.

Blood serum is the straw-colored, watery part of blood that separates from the tiny cells called corpuscles when blood hardens, or *clots*. Koch obtained this fluid from healthy cattle. To get it, he haunted butcher shops and slaughterhouses until he had enough to fill several test tubes.

Then Koch took his test tubes of serum and heated each of them to kill any foreign microbes. Next he set the test tubes on a slant, so that he would have a greater surface of serum on which to sow his bacilli.

When the serum had hardened into a transparent, yellow, jellylike substance, Koch placed on its surface tubercles from a guinea pig that had recently died of tuberculosis. When the last test tube had been treated with the diseased matter, he put them all in an incubator that he kept at the exact temperature of a guinea pig's body.

Day after day Koch watched the slanted test tubes for signs of pure colonies. Nothing happened for two weeks. On the fifteenth day, Koch disgustedly toyed with the idea of throwing the test tubes away. Out of habit, however, he decided to have one last look. Whipping out the little pocket magnifying eyeglass he always kept with him, he held it closely over one of the tubes. There seemed to be some speckled growth on the surface of the serum jelly!

Feverishly, Koch lifted a bit of this growth onto one of his glass slides, stained it with his bluish dye, and looked at it under the microscope. There they were again! The same little crooked blue-stained rods that he had seen time and again in the tissues of animals and men who had died of consumption.

As usual, Koch set to work and produced over forty more cultures of these bacilli before he was satisfied with the evidence.

Now there was one thing left to do: these bacilli, artificially grown outside the body, must give tuberculosis to healthy animals. This Koch proceeded to carry out with relentless thoroughness.

With tubercle bacilli artificially grown from many infected areas, Koch inoculated every healthy animal he could find—rabbits, mice, guinea pigs, chickens, cats, monkeys. He even went so far as to inoculate some creatures that do not ordinarily fall victims to tuberculosis—turtles, eels, frogs, even goldfish!

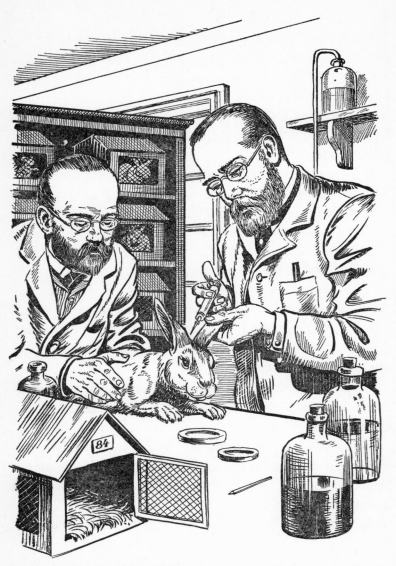

Koch inoculated every healthy animal he could find with tubercle bacilli artificially grown outside the body.

Days, then weeks, went by. Koch's turtles and fish remained perfectly healthy, but the other animals did not. At last, the mice, the guinea pigs, the cats, the chickens began to sicken and their bodies wasted away. After their deaths, Koch thoroughly examined them under his microscope. In every case, the stained bluish rods of tubercle bacilli were found.

Koch's chain of evidence was now complete.

FOURTEEN

Koch Announces
His Great Discovery

THE EVENING of March 24, 1882, was a damp and cheerless one in Berlin. Outside the proud marble building on the banks of the river Spree, it had begun to rain again. The building housed the laboratories and offices of the Health Institute of the University of Berlin. Tonight, the Berlin Physiological Society was to meet to hear Robert Koch make his now famous presentation on the tubercle bacillus.

The Berlin Physiological Society was a small but influential body. Its members insisted that any information presented before it be discussed completely and frankly. Many an ambitious young scientist had had his theories knocked full of holes when he had finished his presentation.

Tonight, the most brilliant men of German science had gathered to listen to Koch. There was the great physiologist, Emil Du Bois-Reymond; and, chatting with him, the famous physicist, Baron von Helmholtz. Paul Ehrlich and Emil von Behring were there, too. So were Cohn and Cohnheim, Gaffky and Loeffler. Even the "professor of professors," Rudolf Virchow, had showed up. Koch, once again swallowing his pride, had invited Virchow to a private demonstration earlier that afternoon, but Virchow had declined to come.

Now the members had begun to gather in the small private library of the Health Institute. The large central table, about which chairs had been placed, was crowded with microscopes and nearly two hundred specimens.

As the room filled, there was a hushed expectancy. Distinguished scientists greeted each other in whispers. Sides that opposed each other were well represented—those who believed in the contagiousness of tuberculosis and those who did not. Helmholtz leaned forward to say something to Du Bois-Reymond. Gaffky and Loeffler, who were to assist Koch, arranged and rearranged specimens. Virchow, smiling and confident, remarked to his neighbor about the "youthfulness" of the work coming from the Health Office these days.

Meanwhile, Koch fiddled with the screws on his microscope and waited. At last, Du Bois-Reymond, who was presiding officer, officially opened the meeting.

When Koch was called upon to speak, he went slowly to his place and pulled some sheets of manuscript from his pocket. Adjusting his gold-rimmed spectacles, he began slowly to speak. At first, the words came with considerable nervousness, even embarrassment. This, after all, the first speech he had made in Berlin—and he was making it before the greatest men in German medicine.

In a short time, Koch had gained control of himself. His voice rose in pitch, his face grew flushed. The audience listened to him with breathless excitement.

Plainly and simply, Robert Koch led his audience with him over his years of work—through all his disappointments and failures—over every step of the ground he himself had covered. Toward the end of his presentation, Koch began to make practical suggestions as to how tuberculosis might be combatted. Those listening to him saw that Koch was making a great deal of sense. Here they were seeing come true the predictions and dreams of men like Koch's old professor, Jacob Henle, and his friend, Julius Cohnheim.

At last Koch made the announcement that everyone had been waiting for: "I have succeeded in discovering the real cause of tuberculosis. It is the tubercle bacillus, a true parasite." By *parasite,* Koch meant that it was a microbe that lives on and gets its food from another living organism—notably human tissue itself.

That night when Koch, with Loeffler and Gaffky beside him, finished reading his amazing paper, all eyes shifted to the great Virchow. But the "professor of professors" simply nodded to Koch, got to his feet and left the room. There was nothing left for him to say.

Nor was there anything that anyone else could say. Koch had succeeded in answering their questions and objections before they had had a chance to speak them. For the first time in the history of the Physiological Society, there was no discussion after a presentation.

"That evening," Paul Ehrlich wrote later, "was engraved in my memory as the most majestic scientific event I have ever participated in."

"There was no one in the room who heard him," said the loyal Loeffler afterwards, ". . . who could be anything

Koch announcing his discovery of the tubercle bacillus as the cause of tuberculosis. Berlin, March 28, 1882.

else but convinced that he had made an epoch-making discovery."

Another eyewitness could not get over the completeness of the evidence Koch had presented—it was all there "right down to the last dot over the last 'i.' "

Seventeen days later, Koch's famous paper—titled *The Etiology* of Tuberculosis*—was published in the *Berlin Clinical Weekly*. As the news of what he had done began to leak out, the name of Robert Koch became a household word. His picture—together with those of Kaiser Wilhelm, Bismarck, and General von Moltke—was printed on red handkerchiefs of which over 100,000 were sold. Verses written about Koch, the "bacillus-father," were printed in daily newspapers.

News of Koch's discovery also began to leak out to the rest of the world. The thirty-year-old Atlantic cable from Europe to America now began to hum with Koch's discovery. Soon Americans from New York to San Francisco were reading the news from across the waters—that a Dr. Koch of Berlin had discovered that a parasite called the tubercle bacillus was the cause of tuberculosis.

Englishmen were reading the same thing in the London *Times*. Soon doctors everywhere, following Koch's lead, were staining the bacilli themselves and studying them. This, of course, proved to be an important weapon against the disease, for, now, if the bacillus could be stained and seen, its presence could be known more quickly. This was an important diagnosis indeed for the killer-disease that took three out of every seven lives.

Robert Koch now found himself to be famous. From

* *Etiology* is the science of investigating the causes of disease.

all over the globe, medical men went to Germany to be able to study under him. In May of 1883, Koch was asked to preside over the Imperial Health Office's pavilion at a large exhibition in Berlin. Here hundreds of people, including many members of European royalty, flocked to hear him lecture on bacteriology.

Fame, however, meant little to Koch. He continued with his work on tuberculosis, hoping to learn more about the disease—perhaps even find a cure for it. And he was now preparing a second and more complete paper on tuberculosis.

This paper, which was not published until 1884, was eighty-eight pages long and contained many excellent photographs of Koch's work on tubercle bacilli and cultures. In this same paper, he also credited the work of other men—contributions without which he could not have made his own discovery of the tubercle bacillus.

In this same medical classic, Koch tells of using, in all, 94 guinea pigs, 44 field mice, and 70 rabbits to prove his final conclusion about tuberculosis. That conclusion rested on three facts: 1. that tubercle bacilli are always present in tuberculosis and occur no place else; 2. that, as true parasites, they are there before the effects of the disease become apparent; and 3. that their number, appearance, and disappearance are in direct relation to the disease's course. Thus Koch could conclude that "with great probability the tubercle bacillus is not a chance accompaniment of tuberculosis, but stands as the direct cause of the disease."

With the publication of this paper, Koch had reached the peak of his fame. Its effects on the prevention, diagnosis, and treatment of tuberculosis was far-reaching. Those who had held that the disease was inherited faded into the background. Sanitarians the world over could then lay plans to combat the killer they now knew was definitely contagious.

Meanwhile Koch had managed to solve one last problem in the life cycle of that deadly bacillus. It was clear to Koch that human beings must catch these bacilli in their systems by *breathing them in* through the air. But could tuberculosis be given to animals in this way?

There was only one way to find out—to actually *spray* the bacilli at some of his animals! It was a dangerous order indeed. When he had been working with cultures alone, he could always dip his hands in the bichloride of mercury to disinfect them. But now—spraying these deadly microbes about in the air! He himself could easily fall victim to tuberculosis.

Nevertheless, Koch went ahead and built a large box into which he could place rabbits, mice and guinea pigs. Into the box he ran a nozzle through which the bacilli could be sprayed by means of a bellows.

For days Koch sat in his laboratory, spraying fine mists of tubercle bacilli. The days stretched into weeks and, sure enough, the pitiful animals began to waste away. Through a little window in the box Koch watched them die one after the other.

Soon, however, Koch was to abandon tuberculosis for another killer. Because once again the dreaded cholera microbe was loose in the world.

FIFTEEN

Cholera in Egypt and India

WHEN Robert Koch had been a young assistant in the General Hospital in Hamburg, he had left certain notes indicating that he must have seen the cholera microbe—without realizing it.

Now, in the summer of 1883, cholera had broken out again in the Near East and was threatening Europe. For centuries a murderer of thousands, cholera originated in and around India. Then it usually spread to southern Europe by way of Egypt or Afghanistan. Naturally, all Europe was terrified when a serious epidemic of the disease suddenly exploded in Alexandria.

With the disease claiming hundreds every week, the alarmed Egyptian government sent out a call to France and Germany for help. Both countries responded immediately. French and German commissions were hastily organized, which soon set sail for Alexandria. Aside from their real desire to track down this microbe, both parties knew it was also a race between Pasteur of France and Koch of Germany to see who would be first.

The French commission arrived on the scene before the German. Pasteur himself, however, had been unable to accompany the expedition because of illness. But he had sent two brilliant, young microbe hunters to head the French commission—Émile Roux and P. Thuillier. Koch himself led the German expedition and took with him his old assistant, Georg Gaffky.

The race was on.

Armed with their microscopes and experimental animals from Berlin, Koch and his party plunged into the gruesome task of examining the bodies of hundreds of dead Egyptians in hospitals and morgues. Into animal after animal, they shot infected material, hoping to produce the disease artificially, but had no success.

Then a peculiar thing happened. The cholera epidemic began to subside as quickly as it had struck. Nevertheless, the French and German commissions worked on, hoping that by an increased effort they could isolate the deadly microbe before the epidemic vanished completely.

The rival cholera hunters avoided each other for the first weeks. Later, however, being on a common mission and strangers in a foreign land, they became friendly. Then one day the Germans became alarmed to learn that the French were packing up for home.

"Do you believe they have found it, Herr Doktor?" Gaffky asked Koch.

Koch replied that he did not know.

The two decided to ask Roux and Thuillier frankly for permission to examine their specimens. This was generously granted by the Frenchmen. Late into the night, Koch studied these specimens, finally realizing that the French had been wrong in thinking they had isolated the disease. They had mistaken blood *platelets*—tiny disks normally occurring in the blood—for the disease-causing microbes.

All rivalry was forgotten next morning, however, when Émile Roux came hurrying to see Dr. Koch. White-faced and trembling, he stammered out the news that Thuillier had an acute—and probably fatal—case of cholera.

Would Koch go to see him?

"*Natürlich*—of course," answered Koch instantly.

When the German bacteriologist arrived at the French commission's headquarters, he found the young French doctor with sunken eyes, obviously dying.

Thuillier looked up at Koch and asked in a weak voice: "Is . . . it . . . the . . . cholera germ?"

"Yes," said Koch, glancing at Roux, "you have found it."

A few minutes later Thuillier died.

At the funeral, which was attended by the German commission, Koch placed two wreaths on the young Frenchman's coffin, saying: "They are simple but they are of laurel, such as are given to the brave."

Koch had landed in Alexandria in August. He and his assistants worked on into September on the cholera problem with scant success. When the epidemic had all but disappeared in Egypt, Koch sent in a request to the Imperial Health Office in Berlin.

Would they allow him to go to India to study cholera there? He had, Koch reported, been finding characteristic microorganisms in the intestinal tissues of victims. In India, always the starting point of the disease, he could investigate further cases; he was sure he was on the right track.

While Koch awaited the decision from Berlin, he investigated sanitary conditions around the northern Red Sea area, which had been so hard hit by cholera. The poor methods he found of fighting cholera there must have made Koch smile. One consisted of having a victim stand for one minute over a mixture of lime, sulphur, dead cholera tissue, and hydrochloric acid. In Suez, another method of fighting cholera was to smoke up the streets with smoldering straw fires—an early attempt at fumigation. Still a third method—which was used on the very boat that carried Koch to Suez—was to spray the bulkheads with a solution of seawater and sulphuric acid, while the walls of the toilet rooms—an excellent breeding ground of cholera —were left unsprayed!

Permission finally came from Berlin for Koch to go to India to carry on his search. Passing through Cairo, he could not resist a visit to the pyramids of Cheops, which he had longed to see since boyhood. From there, he continued through the Indian Ocean, past Ceylon, and finally landed in Calcutta in December of 1883. The long weeks at sea had left him worn out, for he had suffered constant attacks of seasickness.

Exhausted though he was, Koch got right to work in the well-equipped laboratory provided him at the Medical College Hospital in Calcutta. He examined the bodies of dozens of cholera victims and in each one he found bacilli of the same shape as those in the Egyptian victims. In addition, the same microorganism appeared in the intestines of patients sick with cholera. Yet, in no healthy person or animal could Koch find these microbes.

What Koch was seeing through his microscope were

Robert Koch could not resist a visit to the pyramids of Cheops,
which he had longed to see since boyhood.

tiny, crescent-shaped bacilli, shorter than the tubercle bacillus but somewhat thicker. Because of their characteristic shape, Koch called the little boomeranglike sticks *comma bacilli.*

Koch also found that they could be nourished and grown like the tubercle bacillus—on beef broth jelly or blood serum. He grew many cultures of the comma bacillus so that its habits could be studied.

Koch soon found that this murderous microbe would die the moment it was dried or heated sufficiently. It seemed to flourish however in moist, damp, or wet places.

Gradually Koch got at the truth of how cholera spread. He dredged up pail after pail of the foul well water that the Hindus were using for drinking. Here was the swarming home of the comma bacillus and the way it entered the human body. When the victims perished, the disease spread easily to healthy persons via their soiled clothes or bed sheets.

Bad sewage conditions and filthy streets also spread the disease rapidly. In particular, Koch pointed out that unsanitary conditions aboard merchant ships were almost certainly the way cholera could enter a country. The passengers and seamen—even those having stamped health certificates—could easily act as innocent "carriers" of the comma bacillus. But, added Koch, the use of such disinfectants as mercuric chloride or carbolic acid could keep down the spread of cholera.

Nine months after the German commission's arrival in Alexandria, it left for home via Bombay. The newspapers had followed the expedition closely. All Germany was awaiting Koch's return. When he entered Berlin he was treated like a conquering hero. Kaiser Wilhelm himself awarded the famous bacteriologist the Order of the Crown with Star. A proud government gave him 100,000 marks as a reward for his work. Banquets were given in his honor. At one of these in May, a speaker compared the bacteriologist with the heroes of Greek mythology.

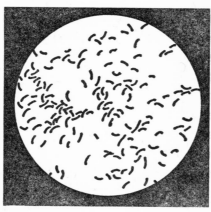

"Comma bacilli" of cholera, as seen through a microscope.

Koch could now report to the medical profession in Berlin that "cholera does not come into being spontaneously —out of nothing." It is a disease that attacks only those who have swallowed the comma bacillus. "And," Koch added, "it is only in a man's intestines, or in highly polluted water such as that of India, that cholera can grow."

Despite his brilliant work and triumphant homecoming, it was to be many more months before Koch's conclusions and recommendations about cholera were to win full acceptance by European doctors. In medical conference after medical conference, Koch explained about the comma bacillus and how it could be stamped out by sensible sanitary precautions. But it was hard to root out old ideas and outmoded laws governing sanitation and vaccination against disease.

One elderly German physician, the well-known Max von Pettenkofer, spoke out repeatedly against Koch. All this talk, insisted Pettenkofer, about microscopic plants and animals causing diseases was nonsense.

Knowing that Koch had brought back from India with him specimens of comma bacilli, Pettenkofer urged his opponent to send him some of them. "Then I will demonstrate how harmless they are," he said.

Koch obliged by sending Pettenkofer a whole test tube full of the vicious, swarming bacilli—enough to cause the deaths of a battalion of men.

Before witnesses, Pettenkofer took the tube and downed the contents at one gulp. Miraculously, nothing happened to him other than a slight sensation of illness. How did Pettenkofer manage to survive this deadly dose? No one could explain it—not even Koch. Today, however, we know that there are deadly germs around us much of the time. They can kill some of us, and leave others unharmed. Pettenkofer was lucky. His system in some mysterious way was not affected by the bacilli.

Despite the success of Pettenkofer's foolhardy experiment, Koch's views won out over his opponents'. New sanitary laws were eventually passed limiting the spread of cholera. Once again, Koch had successfully curbed a dangerous disease.

SIXTEEN

The Discovery of Tuberculin

THE YEARS between 1885 and 1890 were comparatively quiet ones for Robert Koch. For the most part he spent them in further research on tuberculosis and teaching.

After declining a professorship at Leipzig University early in 1885, Koch became the head of the new Hygienic Institute in Berlin; in addition, he was made a full professor at the University of Berlin. He took up his new duties just after the Easter holidays.

Koch was enormously respected now. Many scientific workers in America and other countries sought the opportunity of working under him. One American who came was William Henry Welch, later famous as a medical historian and researcher. Young Dr. Welch was one of those fortunate enough to attend the only complete course on bacteriology that Koch ever gave.

In this course, Koch lectured on the diagnosis and detection of the comma bacillus of cholera. Koch was of the strong opinion that it was unwise to bring any of the cholera germs into Germany, lest somehow they get loose and cause an epidemic. For use in his courses, however,

Koch had had to bring in some of the bacilli from out of the country. The story goes that Dr. Welch had grown some comma bacilli of his own to take back to America with him. Knowing this, Koch fixed his eyes so strongly on Welch in one of his lectures that the young doctor went to his culture, poured disinfectant over it, and threw it into the Spree River.

Another student reported that the usually stern Koch was not entirely without a sense of humor. This young doctor once asked Koch how long a glass slide should be held in a flame when staining the tubercle bacillus. The bacteriologist replied with a smile: "As long as it takes to say, 'Robert Koch is a great man!' " The student was later told that no one at the Institute was permitted to work with, or on, tuberculosis except Koch himself.

Other brilliant young doctors—later to become famous themselves—worked under Koch at this time. There were such Americans as Hermann Michael Biggs, later the noted public health administrator of New York; Walter Reed, famous for his studies of yellow fever; Edward Trudeau, one of the pioneers of open air sanitarium treatment of tubercular patients at Saranac Lake, N.Y.

In addition there were the brilliant Germans—Emil von Behring, who would soon win the Nobel Prize for his work on diphtheria and tetanus; Edwin Klebs, isolator of the diphtheria germ itself; Paul Ehrlich, who would win the battle against syphilis. There was also the serious little Japanese, Shibasaburo Kitasato, who worshipped Koch; later, he would help isolate the tetanus (lockjaw) bacillus with von Behring. Indeed, in his own country, Kitasato was later to become known as "the Japanese Koch."

Although lecturing tended to bore Koch, his new position allowed him to be present at many medical conferences where he could compare notes with noted associates. Koch at this time was in his middle forties, slender, his hair brown, his full beard not yet gray. He was still as nearsighted as ever and seldom removed his gold-rimmed spectacles. Many of the young men under Koch patterned their own beards, mustaches, and clothes after him.

In speaking, his students always found Koch clear and to the point, as he in turn expected them to be. With strangers he was usually quiet, even short-tempered if he suspected they had come to him as mere curiosity seekers. But he was just the opposite with his students and associates, always ready to listen, to advise, to help. He began work early at the Institute and carried on late into the afternoon or evening; those under Koch who wanted to please him did the same. Nevertheless, he enjoyed visiting with his friends and their wives late into the evenings at some tavern or other; here he would astound his companions with his remarkable memory or delight them with stories of his travels.

In 1888, Koch's daughter married one of his associates, Dr. Edwin Pfuhl; the couple left Berlin to live elsewhere, much to Koch's sorrow. At this time, Koch was obliged to spend much time with the German general staff devising plans in case of war. On one occasion, Kaiser Wilhelm even ordered him to attend a meeting in Paris in the full dress uniform of a general. Koch found these obligations extremely tiresome. In addition, he had suffered from a stomach disorder for many months during the year 1888. Nor had his marriage been going especially well, for after his daughter had left their house in Berlin a coolness had sprung up between himself and Emmy.

Any one—or combination of—these reasons may have been the cause of Koch's changing his scientific habits between the years 1889 and 1890. Formerly most agreeable, he now became suspicious and secretive. His students and assistants saw less and less of him. In order not to be disturbed, he began working behind closed doors so that only his closest friends knew what he was doing.

Probably one reason for Koch's irritability was that he was on the track of something big in his battle against tuberculosis, and he resented all interruptions. Indeed, in a few short months Koch was to believe he had found it.

Lately he had noticed a strange thing in some of his experiments. He had injected tubercle bacilli just under the skin of a guinea pig; after about two weeks an ulcer —an open sore that tends not to heal—formed at the site of the injection. The animal later died—but not before Koch had done something else. He inoculated the guinea pig a second time with more tubercle bacilli. At the site of this injection, there was a more rapid, violent reaction; an ulcer formed here, too, but healed promptly! Later, Koch claimed to have tried these inoculations on guinea pigs that were just entering the early stages of tuberculosis. These animals, he said, actually improved in health.

As a result of these experiments, Koch was led to believe that, in the tubercle bacillus itself, there must be some substance that was not only of value in diagnosing tuberculosis—but one that could actually *cure* the disease!

Today medical men call what Koch had done "the Koch phenomenon." From it came the discovery of *tuberculin,* one of Koch's greatest contributions to medicine.

Tuberculin is a liquid product of *sterile*—dead—tubercle bacilli. Koch first prepared it in 1890. First, he sterilized—killed—all the living microbes in the liquid medium in which tubercle bacilli were grown in the laboratory. Then he filtered the liquid and increased its strength by evaporating away some of the fluid mixed with it. Later, using his precise laboratory methods, Koch perfected several types of tuberculin.

At the approach of the Tenth International Medical Conference, to be held in Berlin, Koch began to hope that he had a vaccine against tuberculosis. A *vaccine* is a substance which, when injected into the body, produces immunity to the same kind of bacteria.

No one knew better than Koch himself that he had by no means gone far enough in his experiments to announce *an actual cure for tuberculosis.* Nevertheless, the much-awaited Berlin Conference was getting closer and closer. Should he announce his recent findings?

Certain pressures were probably being put on Koch at this time to do so. In the first place, some word about Koch's new preparation had already leaked out in medical circles; and since Koch was to be a principal speaker at the gathering, he would be expected to reveal any new findings. Also there was his old rivalry with Pasteur who had been announcing new discoveries all along; naturally, the German government urged their own foremost bacteriologist to come forward with anything new. Indeed, it was later rumored that the Kaiser himself had urged Koch to make his premature announcement concerning tuberculin.

However, there is evidence that Koch wished to avoid saying anything at all about tuberculin at this time. Several days before the Conference, he was walking through the streets of Berlin with the well-known anatomist Dr. Wilhelm Waldeyer. Waldeyer later wrote down what they had talked about. Koch was, he said, being constantly badgered by the Minister of Culture and others to reveal his discovery of tuberculin. "Koch then told me," wrote Waldeyer, "that if they continued doing so he would prefer not to make any speech at all."

In the meanwhile, preparations for the Conference were going ahead. Prominent medical men from nearly every country in the world were expected to attend. When the Committee learned that there were to be several thousand, they wondered where they could find a meeting place large enough in Berlin to put them. The site finally chosen was a large barn-like structure in which the famous Renz circus regularly performed. So important did the Committee consider this Conference that they spent days decorating the building like the inside of a Greek temple!

When the Conference opened on August 4, 1890, Robert Koch had, after all, agreed to speak on the subject of tuberculosis.

The anticipation of the audience was pitched high, for the information had gone around that Koch did indeed have some discovery to announce. In fact, the Minister of Culture, who introduced Koch, went so far as to say that certain injections of a substance recently invented by Koch could kill tubercle bacilli—thereby meaning that a cure of tuberculosis had been found!

This, of course, only served to whip up the audience to greater excitement. They could scarcely wait for the celebrated bacteriologist to begin his talk.

But when Koch finally took the rostrum, his statements were extremely careful and moderate. In fact, many in the audience were disappointed. Koch had deliberately chosen a very general title for his speech—"On Bacteriological Research"—and stressed at the very beginning that, to those familiar with his subject, he had nothing especially revolutionary to tell them.

Later on in his speech, however, Koch did turn to his recent studies on tuberculosis. He said that soon after his discovery of the tubercle bacillus, he had been searching for substances that might be remedies for the disease. Moreover, Koch stressed the fact that he *was still continuing* this search constantly.

Then Koch made his now-famous announcement:

"After many failures . . . I finally found substances that proved able to check the growth of tubercle bacilli not only in a test tube, but also in living animals." The "animals" were of course Koch's guinea pigs.

But Koch then followed his announcement with this statement, which clearly indicates that he did not want his words to be misunderstood: "Although these experiments have taken the better part of a year, they are not yet concluded. At this moment, therefore, I can only say this much—that guinea pigs, animals known to be especially prone to tuberculosis, will no longer become infected after inoculation with tubercle bacilli after they have been treated with this substance." In addition, he pointed out that, in other guinea pigs who were in an advanced stage of tuberculosis, the substance seemed to arrest the disease completely—with no damaging side effects to the animals.

Thus Robert Koch clearly warned against drawing too far-reaching conclusions from this discovery. In fact, he voiced the hope that the substance discovered by him might someday prove able to bring about the same results in human beings. Koch added next that, in order to achieve this, he had gone against his usual methods; namely, reporting on experiments that had not yet been brought to a conclusion.

"So," said Koch in conclusion, "let me end my words with the hope that all countries will compete in their efforts in this fight against the smallest, but most dangerous enemy of mankind. . . ."

Yet, no sooner had Koch sat down than his careful and deliberate warnings began to be forgotten. Here was a piece of news the whole world had long waited to hear. It was too big to be held in check. Dammed-up enthusiasm now began to flood around the globe.

The transatlantic cable hummed. Presses rolled out the welcome news. Perhaps no other medical announcement in history produced the sensation that this one did, for it had come directly from "the horse's mouth"—from the very scientist who had himself isolated the tubercle bacillus.

Medical men from all over the civilized world flocked to Berlin to see the effect of the "remedy" and, if possible, to get some to take home. A thousand dollars was freely offered for as little as a teaspoonful of tuberculin; those fortunate enough to have obtained it, however, would not sell at double this price. Crowds paraded the streets of Berlin shouting Koch's name. His picture was glazed on plates and beer steins. Hymns were sung in his honor.

As the news of tuberculin spread, consumptives all over the world began to have fresh hope of recovery. At Trudeau's new sanitarium at Saranac Lake, N.Y., for example, "TB" patients eagerly discussed news reports of Koch's achievement. Feverishly, they asked Dr. Trudeau time and again about the new vaccine.

"I know nothing more of this than you do," Trudeau would answer. "But Koch is a great scientist—he would not announce that he has a cure if he were not sure of it."

Actually, Dr. Trudeau himself had been working along the same lines as his old teacher, but had only partially succeeded in protecting guinea pigs against tuberculosis. However, his natural feeling of disappointment was quickly replaced by genuine joy and praise for the man who had done what he himself had failed to do.

Finally, some patients at Saranac Lake could stand the suspense no longer. Many who were very sick left their blankets and comfortable steamer chairs at the sanitarium and packed up for New York City. By going there, they would be nearer the docks when the American doctors returned with the sought-after tuberculin. Precious days would thus be saved—for some of these patients had not many more days to live.

And so it went. To tubercular patients and their doctors the world over, Koch had become an angel of mercy, his "new cure" a conquering sword.

Then the sad truth began to come out. Tuberculin was not a cure for tuberculosis after all—at least not for human cases. Moreover, doctors were overdosing their patients with it; many in the advanced stages of the disease died. Indeed, Virchow, Koch's old opponent, rashly came out with the statement that tuberculin actually *spread* the disease.

Great resentment now arose against Koch. Abuse was heaped on him from every part of the world. Though greatly upset, Koch remained silent and worked doggedly on. After all, he had been as careful and deliberate in his announcement as a scientist could be. Was it his fault if his warnings had not been heeded, his tuberculin wrongly applied?

Perhaps not. But as the year 1890 drew to a close and he saw his announcement become more and more exaggerated and distorted, Koch felt compelled not to let more false impressions grow. On November 13, 1890, he published a summary on the present state of affairs concerning tuberculin, titled "Further Reports on a Cure for Tuberculosis." In this paper, Koch clarified a number of things. For example, tuberculin must never be taken by mouth, but must be given by injection under the skin. Moreover, man can stand only a small fraction of the substance given to guinea pigs. In far advanced cases, it helps but little. Treatment is best carried out under controlled conditions in a sanitarium.

Koch later re-emphasized the value of tuberculin in diagnosis. He wrote that if a very small quantity of the substance—about 1/10,000 of a teaspoonful—were injected under the skin, many tubercular patients would soon feel as if they had a bad cold, run a fever, and show some kind of reaction at the site of their disease. A healthy man like himself, said Koch, would not react in this way even if ten times such a dose was injected. How did Koch know this? Because he had injected *himself* with it!

Today, tuberculin is still used as a valuable method of diagnosing tuberculosis. In one method, the tuberculin is injected under the skin, as Koch had done. In another—called the *patch test*—a patch soaked with the substance is attached to the skin. If the person being tested has been infected with tubercle bacilli, redness and swelling will develop around the place where the tuberculin was injected—or where the patch was applied.

Although modern medicine had still not found a cure for tuberculosis, Koch remained convinced that in tuberculin he would someday develop one. Ten years later he was still bringing out new tuberculins with that same hope.

SEVENTEEN

A New Job
and Family Difficulties

THE YEAR 1890 had held many disappointments for Robert Koch. Not the least of these was the fact that he and Emmy Koch had been growing farther apart. It was reported that Frau Koch was frequently "difficult" in company, sometimes even hysterical. Formerly a great help to Robert in his work, she had now been out of touch with it for years.

It is highly probable that all this was Koch's fault, for he was not an easy man to live with. When Koch was interested in some problem, he lost all idea of what time it was—or where he was. Thus he would often miss one or two meals a day; lost in thought, he would drift past his own home, but never past the laboratory.

Once he did reach home, he probably took little notice of Emmy. On the other hand, he would lovingly greet his daughter, whom he adored. If Emmy had prepared a meal for him, he would possibly take no notice of it and go right to bed.

There is little doubt that Frau Koch, lonely and neglected, rightfully resented such treatment and complained about it. Irritated by her outbursts, Koch became more and more indifferent to his wife. Then, when Gertrude married and left Berlin, there was less of a home life than ever for Koch to return to at night.

This unfortunate situation dragged on until the year 1893. In June, it reached the breaking point and a divorce was decided on. Previously, Koch had bought and repaired his old home in Clausthal, and it was here that Emmy went to live until her death in 1913. On a wall of this house a tablet in honor of Koch had been placed.

However, when Koch chose to marry again just two months after the divorce, the indignant citizens tore down the tablet. Some of his closest friends refused to speak to Koch because they, too, thought the marriage in bad taste so soon after the divorce.

Actually, Koch happened to meet his future second wife many months before. It was in the year 1890—the same year of his disappointment with the tuberculin announcement. One day, when Koch was having his portrait painted at an artist's studio in Berlin, he saw a painting standing on a nearby easel. It was a picture of a fresh young girl. Koch, fascinated by the subject, asked the artist who she was. The artist replied that she was Fräulein Hedwig Freiberg, one of his most promising students.

The forty-seven-year-old Koch managed to meet this eighteen-year-old artist a short time later. Despite the difference in their ages they fell in love.

During all of his later travels over the globe in search of disease, Hedwig would accompany Koch. She learned how to treat his different moods, how to be of great help to him in his work. Hedwig also proved as brave as she was devoted to Koch. For when she learned that Robert was inoculating himself with tuberculin, Hedwig insisted that he inject her with it too!

With the passing of 1890, Koch decided to take a rest. Bitterly disappointed with the results of tuberculin, overworked and weary, he sailed for Egypt early in 1891. Another matter, too, was troubling the bacteriologist. The Prussian House of Representatives was soon to decide whether certain sums should be given for new medical improvements in Berlin. One of these was to be a possible new Institute for Infectious Diseases, of which Koch would probably be named head. Since infectious diseases were his main interest, Koch anxiously awaited news of this decision.

Meanwhile, the scientist poked about the ruins of Egyptian temples, took trips up the Nile valley—and wrote letters to Hedwig. In April there was welcome news from Berlin. The new Institute was to be set up and Robert Koch was to be its new Director.

Returning to Berlin, Koch took over his new duties in the autumn of 1891. The new Institute was first housed in a three-story apartment building near the Charity Hospital which, because of its unique shape, was called the "triangle." Koch was glad to give up his lecturing in favor of medical research again. Here, too, he had patients under his care once more. These were housed in simple one-story buildings next to the "triangle," which became known as "Koch's barracks."

Hardly had Koch taken over his new position than the dreaded cholera once again invaded Germany. As before,

Hamburg was the city hardest hit by the epidemic; in a few bare weeks, 17,000 cases had developed of which 8,000 were fatal. Because of his famous work on the cause of the disease—the comma bacillus—the city called on Koch's services. Once again, he stressed the importance of diagnosing the illness as early as possible and fighting it with improved sanitary methods.

At the new Institute for Infectious Diseases—later known as the Koch Institute—Koch had once again surrounded himself with able young men from all over the world. Under his supervision and instruction, they eventually returned to their own countries to fight disease. His old assistants, Gaffky and Loeffler, were still with him. So were Edwin Klebs, Paul Ehrlich, and Kitasato.

To most of these men, Koch was entirely devoted. When, for example, Ehrlich had no position in 1890, Koch took him into his laboratory and said, "Do whatever you wish to do." But the great bacteriologist was always a man of strong likes and dislikes. A rift soon developed between him and his brilliant pupil, Emil von Behring.

While von Behring had, in a very short time, found a successful antitoxin for diphtheria and had come far in the study of tetanus, Koch had been failing with his tuberculins in trying to find a cure for tuberculosis. Doubtless this irritated Koch for it looked as though von Behring, his assistant, was outstripping Koch, the master. Also, the balance of the brilliant team Koch had gathered around him was upset by this. The more successful von Behring grew, the more an "inner circle" of those under Koch began to cluster around this younger man.

The result was that von Behring left the Institute in 1894. When some years later, the two men disagreed on the effects of tuberculosis in man and in cattle, Koch refused to have anything more to do with him. Nevertheless, from a distance, the two often did support each other's views with mutual respect.

Moreover, Koch had been carrying on a running feud with Louis Pasteur for years. The great Frenchman and the brilliant German had never tried to conceal their dislike for each other. Pasteur was a showman and regarded himself as a leader of men. Koch was a plodding worker and a careful seeker of facts. Often, Koch saw the weaknesses in Pasteur's work and frankly said so.

Years earlier, at a Geneva Conference on hygiene, Pasteur had challenged Koch to a debate about the use of a vaccine Pasteur had developed against anthrax. Koch rose from his chair, cleared his throat, said that he would rather give his reply in writing, and sat down. Later, Koch purchased some of Pasteur's vaccine in the open market, tested it on sheep, and found it so contaminated that it killed some of the animals.

To Pasteur's credit, however, he never seized the opportunity of attacking Koch when the German's tuberculin failed to cure tuberculosis. Actually, Koch was probably the more jealous of the two men for he always resented the fact that Pasteur was looked upon as the greatest microbe hunter in all Europe—especially since Pasteur was not a physician at all, but a chemist. But while the two were never friends, each doubtless realized the greatness of the other toward the end of their lives.

To add to Koch's difficulties, it was generally known

that—highly respected though he was—he was never quite accepted in Berlin's inner medical circle. For one thing, he was in open conflict with men such as Virchow and Pettenkofer. For another, it was unforgivable at that time in Germany for a former country doctor to have achieved what Koch had achieved when he had not first "gone through the proper channels." This meant advancing slowly through ordinary university positions; it also meant showing the proper respect for, and conduct toward, the senior members of the medical profession. This Koch did not bother to do, and for this reason he remained an outsider.

It was customary, for example, for a comparative newcomer like Koch to call upon the older medical men. Du Bois-Reymond was one of the latter in Berlin at this time. Koch did call upon him, but did not observe the proper etiquette in doing so. Finding Du Bois-Reymond out, he left his card at the older man's home instead of his office, which was not considered correct form. Du Bois-Reymond returned Koch's card to him, refusing to recognize the younger man in this way.

Koch could forget all of these annoyances, however, in hard work. He was now entering the last fifteen years of his life. These were to be spent largely abroad hunting down diseases that were preying on animals and men.

And—here was his chance once again to see the world.

EIGHTEEN

Rinderpest *in South Africa*

ROBERT KOCH'S work on his tuberculins was suddenly interrupted in the year 1896. An urgent call for help had come to him from the British government to help battle the rinderpest in South Africa.

Rinderpest, or "cattle plague," was a disease that was fatal to 90 per cent of the animals it struck. Apparently it had been spreading to the British Cape Colony in South Africa as a result of herds being driven southward from Somaliland. Animals would suddenly come down with chills, heavy breathing, high fever, and a day or so later they would be lying dead.

The telegram to Koch from the alarmed British officials arrived toward the end of October. A month later Koch was in Cape Town, hard at work investigating the disease.

Koch realized immediately that his task was not an easy one. He could neither see the microbes of rinderpest, nor could he succeed in growing them in cultures. Yet, in less than three months, he discovered how the disease could be arrested!

Rinderpest was a *virus* disease. As germs go, a virus is a much smaller microbe than a bacillus; in fact, viruses are so small that they cannot be seen under an ordinary microscope. Even today, there is much to learn about the viruses and scientists constantly study them.

Nevertheless, Koch in the year 1896 was able to determine that the virus of rinderpest lived in the blood and in the gall bladders of infected animals. Further experiments led him to discover how cattle could be made immune to the deadly disease. The vaccine Koch finally developed was a combination of the infected blood of these cattle and a serum of the blood from cattle which had gotten well from rinderpest. He also found that it was possible to make healthy animals immune to rinderpest by injecting them with infected matter from the gall bladders of sick animals.

Thus in February of 1897, Koch could report from Kimberley to the English Colonial authorities that, using his immunization methods, 75 per cent of the cattle in South Africa could be saved from rinderpest. In the Cape Colony alone, this amounted to about two million head.

While he was studying cattle plague in the Cape Colony, news came to Koch that the ancient menace of bubonic plague had broken out in Bombay. When his work on rinderpest was completed, Koch hurried to India to help fight the epidemic. But a German Commission, under Koch's old assistant, Georg Gaffky, was already at work there. Kitasato and Alexander Yersin, another of Koch's famous pupils, had already done important work on the rat-carrying plague. When Koch arrived in Bombay, he had nothing but praise for Gaffky's work, and soon the epidemic was in check. Koch had trained his pupils well indeed!

Presently Koch was off again for Africa. Cases of the bubonic plague had been reported among the colonists in German East Africa. Landing at Dar-es-Salam, he journeyed to Lake Victoria in the interior to study the disease further. At the same time, he managed to find time to investigate other diseases endangering the East African colonists. These included the surra sickness, fatal to horses and camels; Texas Fever, a cattle disease transmitted by ticks; and relapsing fever, a strange disease causing high fever which was transmitted by lice and ticks.

Through his investigation of these diseases, Koch opened up a wide new field of study known as *tropical microbiology*. Perhaps the most valuable of these studies, however, was Koch's growing interest in a new microbe —that of malaria.

For the next three years Robert Koch would track this dangerous marauder over thousands of miles of land and water.

NINETEEN

Koch on the Track of Malaria

WHAT exactly was known about malaria when Koch, still in German East Africa, began to study the disease?

For one thing, it was one of the oldest plagues that had ever troubled mankind. It had killed many of the ancient Greeks; in fact, some authorities still believe that it was a contributing cause of the decay of Greek civilization. This could well be true, for malaria is a disease that attacks the red cells of the blood, bringing on anemia and great weakness. In the case of the Greeks, a nation of people thus weakened could not be expected to carry on a great civilization. Moreover, nearby Italy had been suffering from malaria epidemics for centuries.

Although malaria was highly infectious, doctors in Koch's time were beginning to find out that humans could not pass the disease on to other men directly as, for example, tuberculosis was transmitted. Instead, the microbe was passed on in a cycle—much like a two-way street— from a man to a mosquito, then back to another man.

In the 1890's, Louis Pasteur had established in Paris his

famous Pasteur Institute for the study of parasitic diseases. Among Pasteur's pupils was a young French army surgeon named Alphonse Laveran who had good reason to investigate malaria, for the disease was killing many French colonial soldiers in tropical Africa.

In his studies, Laveran found that a certain parasite was always associated with malaria attacks. He also discovered that this parasite contains a pigment known to be present in the liver of people who have malaria. In 1880, Laveran published a work on malaria called *Paludism* in which he presented a new theory concerning the disease. Paludism means "malarial disease" and comes from the Latin word "marsh." This term was applied to malaria because the disease seemed to break out most often in marshy or swampy areas. Formerly, it was believed that in such marshy places a mysterious kind of air, or vapor, caused malarial attacks. In fact, the word malaria itself comes from the Italian word *mal'aria,* meaning "bad air."

Laveran argued that malaria was caused by a parasite that lived in the blood of the sick person, destroying red blood cells and giving off poisonous substances into the blood stream. But how did this parasite enter the body? For years, it had been suspected that the mosquito transmitted it. Later, the English doctor, Patrick Manson, also came to believe that the mosquito was the transmitter but, despite his brilliant work in other phases of malaria, he never succeeded in explaining how the transmission came about. It remained for the great English physician, Ronald Ross, to clarify the situation. Through his work in India he succeeded in verifying the fact that a mosquito known as the *anopheles* carried the microscopic parasites that cause the disease. Later, Ross succeeded in tracing the whole life cycle of these parasites.

Today, we know that the parasite of malaria belongs to those microbes called *protozoa.* Protozoa are the opposite of bacteria. While bacteria are plant microbes, protozoa are the tiniest known living animals. Part of the malaria microbe's life is spent in the blood stream of a human being and part in the anopheles mosquito. Here is how the cycle works.

The malaria microbes develop to a certain stage in the stomach of the mosquito; next, they move to the glands surrounding the sucking tube (the "stinger") of the insect. When the mosquito bites a person, the microbes enter the person's body in the mosquito's saliva. These microbes multiply very rapidly in the blood cells, finally causing them to burst. The person then feels the chills and fever of malaria.

Finally, when some of the microbes reach a later stage of growth, they are taken into the stomach of any malaria mosquito that bites the sick person. There they undergo further stages of development. Then the whole cycle starts all over again—mosquito to man, man to mosquito, and so on. But, both the body of man and that of the anopheles mosquito are absolutely essential if this parasite is to go on living.

Robert Koch's malaria expeditions began in August of 1898 when he visited the small disease-ridden town of Grosseto, just north of Rome. There he worked out a plan to fight malaria—a plan that would later take him to far-off Java and New Guinea in April of the following year. On this trip to the East Indies, Koch found that it was largely the children who were the carriers of malaria in these tropical islands. Interestingly enough, Paul Ehrlich later wrote that he thought Koch may actually have determined *before* Ross that mosquitoes were the transmitters of the disease!

After visiting Polynesia, Koch again reached Berlin in October of 1900. Hedwig Koch, who had accompanied him on all these trips, had fallen ill in New Guinea, however, and had preceded her husband home.

Koch had been successful in treating patients who had malaria. But how? What plan had he worked out? The answer lay in his perfecting *quinine therapy*. Quinine was the "miracle drug" of the day. Unfortunately, however, it was often wrongly used and not applied at the right stage of a disease.

For example, many physicians only prescribed quinine treatment when the patients showed symptoms of malaria. Those cases that were "latent"—not yet active—were not treated at all. On the other hand, improper treatment with quinine actually *brought on* malaria symptoms! For example, a form of malaria called "blackwater fever" was often caught by persons in this way.

Koch's great work on malaria was the result of an all-important blood test that he developed. By looking at a patient's blood under a microscope, Koch could not only tell what stage the disease was in, but also if a patient had "latent" malaria.

By these tests, Koch came to know just how much quinine was needed for each stage of malaria. In addition, since the test also revealed whether a person was a latent carrier of the disease, he could also give such a person the right amount of quinine to check the parasite's growth in the blood stream.

Dramatic proof of Koch's method of fighting malaria came in 1900. Authorities on Brioni, a tiny island in the Adriatic Sea, had appealed to Koch for help. Brioni was in the grip of a serious malaria epidemic; if aid did not come soon, all 300 inhabitants might die. Koch arrived in November and methodically began to give all 300 his new blood test. The tests revealed that 22 per cent of the Brionians had malaria in one form or another.

By giving his patients just the right amounts of quinine at just the right times, Koch and his assistants were successful in putting down the epidemic. The grateful islanders later erected a monument to Koch, which they hewed out of solid rock in a cliffside.

Returning to Berlin, Koch made preparations to attend the important upcoming First British Tuberculosis Congress in London. While attending this Congress, Koch called attention to the fact that he believed tuberculosis of the chest was caused by air-borne infection. He also managed to start an argument about tuberculosis that raged on for years.

Koch said he was of the opinion that human and cattle (bovine) tubercle bacilli were not the same, and that man had little to fear from the bovine type. Many others, including von Behring, thought otherwise. The result was that the British appointed a Royal Commission to investigate the question. Years later, Koch was proven wrong. The Commission's results showed that bovine tuberculosis was dangerous to man, although it was the human type that was to be most feared.

Honors were now coming thick and fast to Robert Koch. In 1901, the new Kaiser Wilhelm Academy of Science was established and Koch was immediately named a member. In September of 1902, he was elected to membership in the French Academy of Science; oddly enough, the appointment was to fill Rudolf Virchow's place, for the "professor of professors" had recently died. The following year he was chosen an honorary member of the Austrian Academy of Science.

If Koch's previous years resembled an adventure travelogue, the ones remaining to him would be even more so. In December of 1902, he was called upon once again by the British government to investigate outbreaks of "Rhodesian red water fever" in Africa. A disease of cattle, Koch preferred to call it "African Coast fever" since infected cattle transmitted it from the coast to the interior. Koch succeeded in working out a partially effective immunization for this disease.

On this same expedition Koch had more success against a strange disease called the "horse death." The great bacteriologist finally developed a vaccine made from the blood serum of those horses who had recovered from the disease. During this investigation, an incident occurred that shows how tirelessly devoted Koch was to his work.

One morning at 5 o'clock, an assistant awoke to find Koch, fully dressed, bending over him.

"What is it, Herr Doktor?"

"Get dressed, please. We must ride out immediately. A horse has just died of the disease. We'll have to dissect the animal right away."

"But, Herr Doktor," complained the assistant, "could

Robert Koch in Africa on one of his many trips to fight disease there.

it not wait till morning? As a matter of fact, I've been dreaming about dead horses all night."

"Of course, you have," snapped Koch, looking at the man a little amazed. "If you don't dream about these diseases, how do you expect to make progress in curing them?"

Rising promptly at 7 o'clock and driving himself and his staff until well after sundown, Koch stayed on in Africa until mid-1904, investigating other diseases such as recurrent fever and trypanosomiasis. Koch saw to it that his staff was well organized and that each man knew his job. Mobile laboratories were shifted here and there. Special "sections" were set up to study half a dozen different diseases at once. Members of the expedition writing home to Germany spoke of the vultures that waited constantly in the jungle trees to swoop down on abandoned bodies of experimental cattle; in a few hours, only the bones remained. Koch himself was everywhere at once, inspecting first this "section" then another, never seeming to mind the boiling African sun.

In the Rhodesian town of Bulawayo, the bacteriologist celebrated his sixtieth birthday, while at home in Berlin his students read a 700-page tribute to him and unveiled a bust in his honor. During his birthday party in Bulawayo, Koch made an announcement that shocked his fellow workers.

Since 1896, Koch had made one or more trips away from home each year. Now, in 1904, he told his guests that he thought it wise to resign as Director of the Institute for Infectious Diseases in favor of a younger man.

Returning to Berlin in July, Koch's resignation was regretfully accepted. At a farewell dinner, Koch praised the work of his staff and promised them that he would always be available to help them. He himself planned to continue his research in bacteriology independently.

A new building had been erected for the Institute and in it Koch was given a laboratory and an assistant, together with an annual pension of 10,000 marks. Koch was especially pleased when his old friend and assistant, Georg Gaffky, was named to succeed him as Director of the Institute.

But, retired though he was, Koch remained restless. Hardly had 1904 drawn to a close when he was again aboard a steamer for Africa, arriving in Dar-es-Salam early in 1905. Here his investigations centered on three problems—"Red water fever" and trypanosomiasis again, and "relapsing fever." In studying the latter, Koch succeeded in transferring from man to an ape the microbe responsible for the disease. By the end of October, he was back once more in Berlin.

During the remaining six years that Robert Koch lived, he was to spend three of them abroad, fascinated with tropical diseases and indulging to the fullest his desire to travel.

Indeed, this desire was one that Koch never lost.

TWENTY

The Nobel Prize and Work
on Sleeping-Sickness

R OBERT KOCH had always had a certain contempt for honors and awards—even the much valued Nobel Prize. Once, in a letter to a friend, he wrote that he believed the judges were in a bad position "because apparently it matters less to recognize scientific merit than to see that all nations receive their share of the awards." Koch was perhaps a trifle jealous that his younger rival and former student, Emil von Behring, had already won the Nobel Prize. So had other younger men such as David Bruce and an obscure Russian psychologist, Ivan Pavlov.

At any rate, Koch himself won the award in 1905 for distinguished service to medicine. On December 12, he was in Stockholm to receive the prize, and spoke on "How the Fight Against Tuberculosis Now Stands." Here again he emphasized the importance and danger to man of the human type tubercle bacillus compared to the bovine type.

Later that year, the German government decided to send an expedition to eastern Africa to help fight scattered outbreaks of the dreaded "sleeping-sickness." Two years before, an English expedition had investigated the disease under the brilliant leadership of David Bruce, but with incomplete success. Koch was chosen to head the German party since he had done some preliminary studies on sleeping-sickness the previous year.

In May of 1906, Koch arrived at Amani—the first of three camps where he intended to study sleeping-sickness. He would stay here a month, then move on to Mwanza in German East Africa, and finally set up a big camp in the lovely Sese Islands on Lake Victoria.

No one knew better than Koch the danger involved in this mission, for sleeping-sickness was highly contagious and little was known about the microbe that caused it. Bruce had determined that the cause of the disease was a protozoan microbe called a *trypanosome;* and further, that it was transmitted by an insect called the *Glossina papalis,* or tsetse fly. This was all the positive information Koch had to go on.

What was not known was how the tsetse fly transmitted the disease, what food it lived on, and, in fact, whether the insect was the only carrier of the disease or not. If the answers to these questions could be found, all well and good; however, Koch's main mission was to find out how to *fight* the disease for it was claiming a terrific number of lives.

At Amani the year before, Koch had left a skeleton crew of workers to do research work on, among other things, the tsetse fly. These men had not been idle. They had found out that the insect would normally live only a few days in captivity; however, they had worked out certain techniques for breeding them and keeping them alive for months. Thus Koch had an opportunity to study these insects closely.

The more he and his assistants studied the tsetse fly, the more they became convinced that it lived solely on blood. But what kind of blood? Later, after examining the stomachs of more than 1,000 flies, it was determined that they fed on the blood of crocodiles.

At Mwanza, Koch had plenty of thrills shooting crocodiles, but when he took blood samples from the reptiles the sleeping-sickness microbe itself was not present! To add to his difficulties, Hedwig Koch, who accompanied him on all these trips, came down with malaria and had to return to Berlin.

Koch next moved on to the Sese Islands in British East Africa, where there was much sleeping-sickness. Until recently, these peaceful islands had been a paradise for those who inhabited them. Coffee, banana, and citrus trees grew in fertile plenty. No wild animals roamed the islands except some small antelope. Gentle and unwarlike, these islanders had once had a population of 35,000, but in a short time the sleeping-sickness had wiped out more than 20,000 of them!

The islands themselves were hilly and the people lived on the lofty slopes, high above Lake Victoria. But ringing the islands down near the water were thick jungles in whose shade lived countless numbers of *glossina*—tsetse flies. When fishermen descended through the jungle to the lake, when hunters hunted the antelope there, when women gathered firewood, the deadly flies—as hungry for human blood as for crocodile—bit and infected them.

To make matters worse, sleeping-sickness often did not

develop in a person bitten for weeks, months, or even years. Thus, these infected people would carry on their normal occupations and come in contact with others—spreading the disease even further. Some infected natives often became so insanely violent that the rest of the community protected themselves against them with spears.

Koch set up his camp on high ground and built a makeshift hospital where he cared for as many infected patients as he could. In handling over a thousand cases of sleeping-sickness, Koch came to recognize that the disease usually went through three clear-cut stages. In stage one, the trypanosomes were only found in the blood of the patient, who often ran a high fever. In the second stage, the microbes swelled the glands, particularly those of the throat and neck. The third stage began when the trypanosomes invaded the brain and could be traced in the patient's spinal fluid.

It is from the third stage that sleeping-sickness gets its name. The victim suffers headaches, cannot move certain muscles, feels so tired that he sleeps or dozes for long periods of time. Naturally, if he is asleep most of the time he cannot eat enough food to keep up his strength; his body gets thin and loses flesh. If the victim in this condition is allowed to go unattended, he eventually falls into a sleep so deep that he never wakes up.

Koch was able to make several practical suggestions for fighting this disease. First, destroy the murderous flies by cutting down and clearing the worst of the jungle breeding grounds; then, sow other plants that would keep down the shady undergrowth that the insects liked. Destroy or drive away the crocodiles on whose blood the insects thrived. Kill the microbes in human beings by catching the disease in its earlier stages and dosing the patients with *atoxyl.*

Once again, Koch had worked out a blood test that told him in which of the stages of sleeping-sickness his patients were. When Koch knew this, he knew how much atoxyl to administer. *Atoxyl,* an arsenic preparation, had been used before in sleeping-sickness, but with varying results. Now, by testing his patients' blood, Koch increased the atoxyl doses at precisely the time when they would do the most good.

When the stricken islanders found out that Koch had a remedy for sleeping-sickness, they came in such numbers for treatment that it was necessary for the German commission to build a stockade around their camp. Working day and night, Koch and his assistants treated as many of the natives as they could. Finally, after months of work at Lake Victoria, the Germans succeeded in cutting down the death rate of sleeping-sickness by more than 90 per cent!

In November of 1907, Robert Koch returned to Berlin. Again he was welcomed home as a hero. Everywhere he was honored and treated with enormous respect. In Berlin's Kaiserin-Friedrich Haus, the Kaiser himself came to hear Koch lecture on his experiences at Lake Victoria. In recognition for his services to Germany and the world, Koch was given the special title of Civil Servant Extraordinary which, together with other privileges, meant that now he would be addressed as "Your Excellency."

While Koch had been away in Africa, there had been talk of setting up the Robert Koch Foundation for Com-

Koch in the Sese Islands on Lake Victoria, Africa, 1906–7. His German commission cut down the death-rate of sleeping-sickness there by more than 90 per cent.

bating Tuberculosis. Shortly after Koch's return, this Foundation came into being. Contributions poured in from all over the world. The American millionaire, Andrew Carnegie, contributed the sum of 500,000 marks, which was matched by the German government. Those who contributed 10,000 marks or more had their names inscribed in the Robert Koch "Golden Book" at the Foundation.

It was now the year 1908. Robert Koch was still restless. In all his travels, he had never actually circled the globe. This he decided to do.

TWENTY-ONE

Koch in America
and Japan

I N THE SPRING of 1908, Robert Koch left Berlin on his last great trip. Stopping briefly in London to take part in a conference on sleeping-sickness, he was soon on his way toward North America. In the United States, he planned to visit his brothers, one of whom was a farmer in Iowa.

On April 7, Koch's ship docked in New York. When he came down the gangplank, newspaper reporters crowded about him, begging for an interview. Koch, feeling peppery and a bit irritated, muttered under his breath that they were all "lice-pickers." Nevertheless, the reporters, surprised to hear the great bacteriologist speaking almost-perfect English, got their story.

Immediately the famous German doctor was whisked off to the Academy of Medicine where he was made an honorary member. Two days later, the Academy and the German Medical Society gave a large dinner in Koch's honor at the luxurious Waldorf Astoria Hotel. Many of the most prominent men of American medicine were present, as well as Andrew Carnegie who had contributed so generously to the Koch Foundation in Berlin.

Fidgeting in his chair at the Waldorf dinner, Koch listened to the many speeches praising him and his work. Rising, Koch replied in part to these compliments:

". . . am I really entitled to such homage? . . . I have done nothing else than what all of you are doing every day. I have worked as hard as I could and fulfilled my duty and obligations. If my success was really greater than is usually the case, the reason is . . . that I came in my wanderings through the medical field upon regions where gold was still lying by the wayside. And, while it is necessary to be able to tell gold from the base metals, that is still no great achievement."

Koch ended his speech with a special word of thanks to Andrew Carnegie, and the hope that the Robert Koch Foundation would fight tuberculosis to the benefit of all mankind.

After inspecting the laboratories of the New York City Board of Health under his old pupil Hermann Biggs, Koch left for the Middle West where he visited his brothers. As usual, his wife, Hedwig, went with him.

But Koch did not linger long in the United States. It had always been a favorite dream of his to visit the exotic land of Japan. In June of 1908, he sailed for that country. Before landing there in July, Koch stopped at the Hawaiian Islands in the Pacific, where he visited the leper colony at Molokai.

Koch's former pupil, the now-famous Baron Kitasato, awaited him in Japan. For more than fifteen years, the two had not met and they greeted each other warmly. The

German bacteriologist was in no way disappointed in Kitasato's homeland; in fact, he fell in love with its ways and its people. So much so that many times during his stay there, Koch took to wearing a richly embroidered Japanese kimono.

From the very moment that he stepped off the steamer *Liberia Maru* at Yokohama, Koch was looked upon—and treated very much like—a god. A former pupil of Koch's, Professor M. Miyajima, adoringly reported that "Koch, now in his sixty-fifth year, was completely bald; the powerful shape of his head reminds one a great deal of that of Confucius."

Worshipfully, the Japanese scientists called the great bacteriologist "Father." Koch was wined and dined everywhere he went. A Shinto temple was built in his honor at Kitasato's Institute in Tokyo, where Koch was welcomed like an Imperial prince. The story also goes that Kitasato, observing that Koch was in the habit of trimming what was left of his sparse hair, saved some of the strands and after Koch's death placed them in the Shinto temple.

Koch was also delighted when Kitasato showed him an unusual method of Japanese fishing, in the Agyu-nagara River. Kitasato had often told Koch of this in Berlin, but Koch had refused to believe it. Aboard the boat, the fishermen attached a number of hawklike birds called cormorants on lines. The birds would plunge into the river and guzzle as many fish as they could. They were then hauled aboard and choked so that they disgorged the fish. Astonished, Koch suddenly picked up some fish and threw them back overboard. Again the birds caught them in the

Koch in Japan. Due to his bacteriological achievements, he was almost worshipped in this country.

same unusual way. Like a child, Koch clapped his hands enthusiastically.

Charmed and fascinated by Japan, Koch basked in the attention of its people for nearly six weeks. His stay was interrupted, however, when Kaiser Wilhelm and some American medical men brought pressure on him to represent Germany at the Washington International Congress on Tuberculosis. Koch had planned to go on to China, then continue his round-the-world journey across Asia into Europe and home to Berlin. Reluctantly, Koch now had to abandon this plan and sail all the way back across the Pacific to the United States.

He was in a hot temper when he arrived there. More than once, Koch complained of the too-frequent lunches and dinners, and of the too-strenuous activities—among them attending American boxing matches!

Preceding the Congress, the city of Philadelphia entertained Koch at a banquet; guests paid ten dollars a plate —a good bit of money in 1908. At this banquet, Koch met some American doctors who told him of some work they had done on developing an immunity against tuberculosis. This might be done, they said, by inoculating animals with increasing numbers of tubercle bacilli, beginning with one tubercle bacillus.

"Nonsense!" declared Koch. "No one can isolate a single tubercle bacillus."

The Americans replied that they had employed a new technique, developed by the noted Professor Barber of California, for isolating single yeast cells.

"That might be possible," admitted Koch. "But a single tubercle bacillus—never."

"But Your Excellency," the Americans insisted, "we have already succeeded in isolating a single influenza bacillus."

Koch would have none of it. But the Americans, feeling that the presentation of their work at the Washington Congress might receive a serious set-back with Koch in this mood, offered to send for Professor Barber to demonstrate the technique. This was later done in Washington and Koch was finally convinced.

Even being named Honorary President of the Washington Tuberculosis Congress did not improve Koch's already ruffled temper. He still defended his old belief that bovine tuberculosis was comparatively harmless to human beings—although he was less insistent on it than he had been years before. Nevertheless, he challenged anyone to prove that bovine tubercle bacilli could be found in cases of chest tuberculosis.

Politely, no one did. The members of the Congress knew Koch was there against his will, and a diplomatic statement was given out to the newspapers to which few could object. Right or wrong in his views, however, Koch had been the central figure at the meeting. Such men as Trudeau, Theobald Smith, and William Welch listened to Koch with the greatest respect. Even President Theodore Roosevelt had popped in once at the meeting to hear the great bacteriologist speak.

Robert Koch never completed his trip around the world but returned to Berlin. As usual he concentrated on his favorite work—problems having to do with tuberculosis.

In February of 1910, Koch celebrated the sixtieth birthday of his old assistant, Georg Gaffky. And, on April 17 he gave his last address before the Academy of Science, in which he stressed the necessity of caring for individual tuberculosis patients and of proper hygienic methods for preventing the spread of the disease.

But even as he sat down amid the applause of old friends and devoted pupils, Koch knew that time was running out.

TWENTY-TWO

Last Days

O NLY the inner circle of Robert Koch's friends and fellow workers really came to appreciate the scientist's great charm. Outwardly often testy and overbearing, he remained a real friend to those closest to him. He was at his best in discussion groups—always ready to answer an argument in the precise, clear statements for which he was famous. By profession a doctor, he often astonished those about him with his wide knowledge of other subjects—botany, physics, mathematics, zoology, chemistry, geology, anthropology, and many more.

Those who knew Koch best knew him for a simple, unpretending man. He hated congresses and "occasions." He cared little for the honors that emperors, princes, kings, and scientific bodies heaped upon him. And—Koch had had the highest of these and many, many of them. Yet he really had little need of these honors, for his own work would always stand as a far greater monument than his many medals and ribbons.

Robert Koch had discovered the tubercle bacillus, the cholera microbe, the germ of Egyptian ophthalmia; proved the anthrax bacillus the cause of anthrax, made notable contributions to victories gained over malaria, sleeping-sickness, bubonic plague, rinderpest, leprosy, blackwater and red water fever, surra sickness and Texas fever. In disease, Koch had earned one excellent reputation after another—so that even today the full significance of his work is still not known. Some scientists have estimated that Koch added to the knowledge of half a hundred diseases of men and animals!

Moreover, those closest to Koch admired him for the ideal scientific worker that he was. They admired the severe way he himself criticized his own work; the high intelligence he brought to every problem; the inventiveness he used in overcoming great obstacles. Perhaps most of all they admired his great courage and constant hard work in sticking to something where other scientists had failed.

Even in failure itself, Koch's friends could not help but respect him. As the years passed and his pupils began to see that there could be no cure for tuberculosis, Koch still continued to develop new tuberculins—still hoping that the next one would be the cure that he was looking for.

But as the first decade of the twentieth century drew to a close, Koch's circle of friends saw little signs that he was weakening. It was only a question of time how long Koch could remain among them.

As early as 1903 the bacteriologist had written his daughter from Africa that he thought that he must soon retire. Although he was only sixty at that time and felt well, he had noticed "little hints" of approaching old age —and heart trouble.

Later in 1907, while fighting sleeping-sickness in the

Sese Islands, he had been standing on a high hill looking down on Lake Victoria. Without warning, he felt a terrible wrench in the region of his heart. Such a dizziness swept over him that he almost collapsed.

A year later in Japan, he had been out on a morning climbing party on the island of Myashina when a similar attack made him too weak and dizzy to walk. Reluctantly, he had allowed himself to be carried back to the inn where he was staying.

In March of 1910, Koch suffered signs of *angina pectoris*—a painful disease characterized by a sense of suffocation in the chest. A month later, in April, another attack nearly killed him.

After eating a light meal with his wife, Koch had retired. Suddenly, near midnight, Koch awoke in a high sweat and with such wracking pains and shortness of breath that he believed himself "completely destroyed." His physician was called and Koch was given morphine injections. These, together with strong coffee and compresses applied to his chest, brought the scientist around.

In May, Koch seemed to rally again. He was allowed to leave his bed for short periods of time. Although he was terribly weak, Koch still insisted on working. He asked for the latest news at the Institute. He talked of a new building to care for more tuberculosis patients.

Still peppery and outspoken, Koch now demanded that his physicians allow him to visit the country where he could enjoy green woods and fresher air. His doctors saw the handwriting on the wall, shook their heads, and granted permission. A friend commented: "A man like Koch either lives the way he wants to, or not at all."

In the middle of May, Koch, with great exertion, visited his daughter. Both believed it would be the last time they would see each other.

They were right.

Together with his wife and his personal secretary, Bernhard Möllers, Koch went to the old watering town of Baden-Baden. Arriving on May 20, the scientist was in a cheerful mood and hoped that he might regain full health by treatment in a new sanitarium there.

On the evening of May 27, at the suggestion of Hedwig Koch, he dressed for dinner and sat down for a moment in a comfortable chair. His wife and Herr Möllers left the room for a few minutes. Koch's chair was on the threshold of the hotel balcony. The door was thrown wide open and Koch was watching a glorious sunset dipping lower and lower over the Oos Valley.

Suddenly, his chin dropped on his chest. When Möllers found him, he saw that there had been no pain—no struggle. Koch had slipped away peacefully.

According to his own wishes, the body of Robert Koch was cremated at Baden-Baden on May 30, 1910. Besides his wife, only a few close friends were present, among them Gaffky, Möllers, and Paul Ehrlich. His ashes were placed in an urn, which now rests in a niche behind a marble tablet in his honor at the Robert Koch Institute. After his death, which was mourned by all nations, one English newspaper seemed to speak for the world when it said: "The death of Robert Koch is a loss not only to Germany; all mankind is the poorer."

More than three decades after Koch's death, Berlin was bombed around the clock by the Allies in World War II. At the war's end, ruins and destruction were everywhere. But oddly enough, in the midst of those ruins, Koch's Institute and the mausoleum containing his remains were untouched—as if a greater hand had wished the scientist's resting place left undisturbed.

Glossary of Bacteriological and Medical Terms

ANEMIA—a condition in which the red blood cells are reduced in number or deficient in hemoglobin, causing paleness and shortness of breath.

BACILLI—rod-shaped bacteria. Bacilli are also called germs or microbes.

BACILLUS—a single rod-shaped bacterium.

BACTERIA—a group of one-celled plant microbes having no definite nucleus, or center. They are the opposite of protozoa, which are one-celled animals. Bacteria are so small they can only be seen with the aid of a microscope. Some are harmless, some are useful, and some cause disease.

BACTERIOLOGY—the science which deals with the study of bacteria.

BACTERIUM—a single one-celled plant microbe.

BLOOD SERUM—the watery part of the blood separated from the solid part; especially such a liquid obtained from the blood and used to prevent or cure disease.

CLOT—the thickening of blood, as in a wound.

COLONY—a group of microbes of one kind growing closely together.

COMMUNICABLE DISEASE—a disease that can be given or passed on; a contagious or "catching" disease.

CONSTITUTIONAL DISEASE—a disease that is inherited; for example, one that is passed on from a father to his son.

CONTAGIOUS DISEASE—a disease passed from one person to another as a result of some contact between them.

CONTAMINATE—to soil, make impure, or render unfit for use; for example, a water supply or sewage system by the introduction of harmful bacteria.

CULTURE—a cultivated or specially prepared growth of microorganisms, such as bacteria.

CULTURE MEDIUM—the food or nourishment on which a culture is grown.

DIAGNOSIS—recognizing or being able to correctly name a disease from its symptoms.

DISINFECTANT—any of several chemical preparations used to destroy disease germs or other harmful microorganisms.

EPIDEMIC—a rapidly spreading attack of disease affecting many people.

ETIOLOGY—the investigation of the causes of disease.

FUMIGATION—a method of disinfecting an area by applying smoke, vapor, or gas.

GALL BLADDER—a muscular sac, present in most animals, that stores up the bile from the liver until it is needed. Bile is greenish fluid that aids in digestion.

GERM—any microorganism, especially the harmful bacteria; a microbe.

GLAND—an organ in the body that prepares a substance to be used by the body or discharged from it; for example, the salivary gland.

HYGIENE—the science that studies and explains the facts about health.

HYGIENIC—of or having to do with health; sanitary.

IMMUNITY—safety or protection from a disease, as by vaccination.

INCUBATOR—in bacteriology, a device that supplies the necessary heat to hatch microorganisms.

INFECTIOUS—capable of spreading to others, as an infectious or "catching" disease.

INJECTION—the forcing of a fluid into the body—usually by a syringe—for the purpose of relieving pain or protecting against disease.

INOCULATION—the act of giving a disease to a person or an animal, in a very mild form, for the purpose of preventing a further attack of that disease, by producing immunity.

LATENT PERIOD (of a disease)—the time in which a disease is present, but does not actively show itself.

MICROBE—a plant (bacterium) or animal (protozoan) so small that it can only be seen through a microscope; a microorganism; a germ, especially the harmful kind.

MICROORGANISM—a plant or animal so small that it can only be seen with a microscope (or one that cannot be, such as a virus) ; a germ or microbe.

MICROPHOTOGRAPHY—the process of photographing microscopically small living subjects, such as bacilli.

PARASITE—a tiny plant or animal that gets food from, or lives on, another plant or animal (called the *host*).

PATHOLOGIST—a specialist in pathology.

PATHOLOGY—the science of treating diseases, and finding out what their natures and causes are.

PLATELET—tiny, platelike discs normally found in the blood of mammals.

PROTOZOA—tiny, single-celled animals—the lowest form of animal life. The opposite of bacteria, which are one-celled plants.

SANITARIUM—a health retreat or institution for the recuperation and treatment of diseased persons, usually located in the mountains.

SERUM—see BLOOD SERUM.

SPLEEN—a glandlike organ near the stomach or intestines of most animals.

STERILIZE—to free from living germs; disinfect.

SYMPTOM—any noticeable change or sign in the bodily functions that indicates disease.

SYRINGE—a small pump with a hollow needle for cleaning wounds or injecting fluids into the body.

THERAPY—the treatment of disease.

VACCINATION—the process of giving a very light form of a

disease to a person by injecting a vaccine into the body to prevent a serious attack of the disease.

VACCINE—in general, any substance for preventive inoculation; for example, dead bacteria injected into the body to bring about immunity to a disease.

VIRUS—any of a group of several extremely tiny microorganisms. They are much smaller than bacteria and cannot be seen under an ordinary microscope. So far, scientists know only of the harmful ones causing disease. Viruses are parasites that live and multiply only in the living cells of man, animals, plants, or even other microbes. Some scientists believe viruses are too small to be considered either plants or animals.

Index